Seven Steps to Developing Your Intuitive Powers

D0964948

About the Authors

BETTY BETHARDS is a widely known psychic, mystic, healer, and author of eight books including the bestselling, *The Dream Book: Symbols for Self-Understanding*. She is the president of the non-profit Inner Light Foundation, which she founded in 1969. Through her numerous TV, radio, and media appearances, she has helped millions of people in their search for self-knowledge.

Betty has been affectionately called "The Common Sense Guru." She has lectured throughout the U.S., Canada, Japan, and Australia helping people tap into their intuitive abilities by using the powerful, yet simple tools of dreams, meditation, and visualizations. She offers ongoing lectures, workshops, seminars, and weekly classes in the San Francisco Bay Area.

Betty's teachings come from her attunement to her inner Guidance or spiritual teachers. She believes we all can tap into this intuitional level of insight and wisdom by learning to listen within. Her mystically inspired teachings have a positive down-to-earth message for everyone. The weekly class on which this workbook is based has inspired tremendous spiritual growth. Betty hopes the same magnificent rewards will now be part of your spiritual journey.

Enjoy the awakening!

JACLYN GRACE is the vice-president of the Inner Light Foundation and author of a children's book, *Clarence Honeybear Shines His Inner Light*. She has worked with Betty since 1985 in helping to organize and arrange her seminars, workshop materials, and media appearances.

Seven Steps to Developing Your Intuitive Powers

An Interactive Workbook by

BETTY BETHARDS
AND
JACLYN GRACE

ELEMENT

Boston, Massachusetts • Shaftesbury, Dorset
Melbourne, Victoria

© Element Books, Inc. 1998
Text © Betty Bethards and Jaclyn Grace 1995

First published as *The Way of the Mystic* in the USA in 1995 by
Element Books, Inc.

This edition first published in the USA in 1998 by
Element Books, Inc.
160 North Washington Street, Boston, MA 02114

Published in Great Britain in 1998 by
Element Books Limited
Shaftesbury, Dorset SP7 8BP

Published in Australia in 1998 by
Element Books
distributed by Penguin Australia Limited
487 Maroondah Highway, Ringwood, Victoria 3134

Reprinted 1999

Cover design by Slatter-Anderson
Printed in the United States by Courier Westford, Inc.

Library of Congress Cataloging in Publication data available.
British Library Cataloguing in Publication data available.

ISBN 1-86204-249-7

Dedication

To all the classmates of my Monday Night Live
Courses over the many years. Seeing the lights
come on in your eyes and the magnificent changes
that have occurred in your lives inspired me to take
this workbook out to the world.

. . . and to my dear husband, Charles Rubin

Acknowledgments

I want to express my thanks and appreciation to several people who really assisted in the creation of this work: Paul Cash, for his guidance, wisdom, and flexibility; Dr. Cary Howard for her wonderful input, educational materials, and ideas throughout the years in support of the Inner Light Foundation and myself; MaryGale Beyer, Merriam Wakakuwa, and Susan Pinelli for their computer and transcribing help; and Neal Grace for his editing suggestions.

A special thank-you to the staff of Element Books for their dedication and zest for bringing this book to fruition.

Contents

How to Use this Book

Seven Steps to Developing Your Intuitive Powers was designed from a seven-week class model. In using the workbook, we suggest that you proceed at a pace and flow which best suits you. We do, however, have some recommendations that we have found to be the most useful and effective for reaping the benefits of this course.

As you begin, be sure to complete the reading of each week's text before doing the exercises that follow. The course is best done in a sequential fashion, as each week's lessons are designed to further deepen and enrich the information previously studied. You can complete each step on a weekly basis or you may wish to take longer with certain topics. If so, please continue using the daily tools of meditation, visualizations, and dreams, as these are essential ingredients for the development of your intuitive abilities and spiritual insights.

Week 1

TAPPING YOUR HOTLINE
TO THE DIVINE

What lies behind us and what lies before us are small matters compared to what lies within us.

—Ralph Waldo Emerson

Becoming a Mystic

From the beginning of time, humankind has had a direct line to the divine mind. Each of us has an inner treasure map with a marked path to lead us to our ultimate destination. We know exactly how to bring forth our merger with the God Self. When we hear truth, we recognize it immediately and understand. Some of us feel goose bumps or chills going up our spines—and others, just a heart-felt hit that says, "I knew that."

When we understand that this map that lies within us always contains the perfect direction we need to be taking in our lives, we begin to develop our abilities to tap a higher source of guidance and insight. This is the beginning of the mystical journey. Some of us may choose to walk a path dedicated to self-growth while others follow pathways that avoid taking responsibility. But each of has a unique and clear path to divine consciousness when we choose it.

This life is a wonderful opportunity we have chosen for our soul to gain the wisdom, understanding and realization of the oneness of all life. We gain complete freedom as we develop the mystical perception and see that no one can hurt us, use us or criticize us unless we set them up to do so. We have tremendous power to create a rich, loving, and harmonious life filled with abundance.

Definition of the Mystic

A mystic is one who believes in a direct, intimate union of the soul with God through one's life practice and love. The mystic is actively involved in an ongoing process of changing the ordinary self into the Higher Self. He or she participates in the world from the perspective that God is everything and lives and works to reunite the body, mind, and spirit with the divine force.

Mystics believe we each have total responsibility to create our reality by our thoughts, words, and actions. We are the architect and builder of our lives and we're getting out of life exactly what we think we deserve—nothing more, nothing less. If we don't like how our lives are going, we can keep what we do like and change what we don't. This is a moment by moment, hour by hour self-observation practice. Life is our temple to demonstrate our consistent and devotional relationship to God.

The mystical perspective removes all blame from others and sees life as a reflection of what's inside the individual. Becoming a mystic means moving into a whole new understanding of the nature of our relationship to God. It answers such questions as "Who am I? Why am I here? What is my life all about? What is my purpose? Does a relationship to God mean that we turn all of our problems over to God and let God resolve them? Or does it mean that we try to perceive truth and honestly resolve the fears within ourselves with God's help?"

Most people try to keep busy to avoid facing these questions, whereas the mystic dives into the exploration of all these questions, searching deeply within the self to receive the answers to facilitate growth. Walking the spiritual path leads us to the desire to merge ourselves with the God source. We work to transform our lives by becoming direct co-creators with God in our daily experiences, rather than remain a "separate self" who is still identified with being set apart from this divine power.

Life as School

Each person and situation we encounter becomes our teacher. Part of the mystical teachings I was given is that we choose the life patterns and relationships we encounter. Before incarnating we selected our parents, race, sex, time and date of birth, and the lessons of the first twenty-eight years of our lives. These were wisely selected in order to erase past karma situations and walk through any fears to release them.

Whatever our circumstances, we created them. We didn't choose them in order to suffer. We chose them to learn *how to* and *how not to* relate to our life situations. Unfortunately, many people who were raised with a dysfunctional parent turn around and enact the same behavior patterns when they're an adult, rather than learn from example that these negative behaviors are self-destructive. In identifying the patterns, we can release them and create new patterns of self-worth.

These challenging experiences also build our inner strengths. Mental, physical, and sexual abuse, the death of a child, diseases, illnesses, and accidents are all opportunities to gain deeper wisdom and insight into the true nature of life. If we chose anything less than a perfect body, it was for a reason; it was never to punish, only to teach. Everything we perceive of as suffering is really a wonderful opportunity to correct past mistakes or imbalances and move toward our ultimate goal of enlightenment.

Once we get the idea that we have created our own situation here in the Earth school, we are able to ask why. "What is my positive lesson? What is this teaching me?" Then at last, we stop blaming others for our unhappiness and realize no one else can limit our lives. We cannot change others, but we can change ourselves and move beyond any given situation.

For myself, it took me two years to accept the idea of reincarnation after my Guidance taught me. I believe God is a loving force, and it finally made complete sense to me that we come to the Earth to work out our lessons, release and heal ourselves from the choices and mistakes made in our past lives. Also, we have incarnated to develop our intuitive abilities and talents to know and love ourselves in our true unlimited form.

If I did not believe this, I'd ask myself, "What kind of God would it be if this was our only life and people had to be born blind or starving and crippled in some form or another? What sense would that make?"

Our Team of Teachers

We all have a Guardian Angel and a team of teachers who direct and guide us throughout our lives. God does not trust us down here alone! We know that Catholics are supposed to have a Guardian Angel, but in truth, everyone does. These are beings who have never incarnated on Earth but possess a vast knowledge in helping to oversee our journey.

The Guardian Angel records our life story so when we cross over at the time of death, we are given a videotape to review entire earthly experience. When we see life from this perspective, we can't blame anyone else for our situations because we will realize that they were all our creations.

The team of teachers, which I call our Guidance, are beings who have already completed their human spiritual journey on the Earth plane and are now serving to guide us along on our journey home. They are there to help set up all the lessons our souls are yearning to learn. They love us unconditionally, which is far more than we love ourselves.

We have known these teachers in many previous lifetimes. They are the ones who will greet us and review our life story with us when we cross over at the time of death. They love us but are very detached and don't pamper us when we get into our self-pity numbers or into denial about what's going on. They wait patiently for us to get back to our centers and find the lesson being shown.

Their help makes our journey on Earth much easier when we learn to tap this source for help and direction. We always have free will to make our own choices, but our Guides are there twenty-four hours a day to help us when we need it. We each have three teachers who accompany us throughout our entire lifetime. Others will assist as needed, depending on the type of growth we're accomplishing.

Everyone prays for help but nobody ever stops to listen! It is only when the mind is focused to one point that we can actually hear our Guidance and receive new ideas. We may have experienced this when we were doing long distance driving at night. Our minds are focused on the road and we get all kinds of insights and ideas. That's our Guidance.

We may at one time have had a car accident when time and space seemed to slow down and we were guided by an inner voice and told how to handle the crisis calmly and easily to avoid further danger. We were lifted partially out of the body. In this state our Guidance can speak directly to us.

A being who is our teacher must qualify by being wiser than ourselves. That's why when we need help, I recommend asking our Guidance or God directly rather than asking a deceased friend or relative for insight. Just because people have died, doesn't mean that they are wiser than us. They can, however, send us love and support. I see many people who start developing their spirituality and become fascinated and stuck in their psychic level of understanding.

The psychic level is a limited realm that doesn't necessarily impart any greater self-understanding for us. It shows us that other realities exist beyond the physical realm, but it's far more important to develop our mystical abilities, which allow us to co-create directly with God. Going beyond psychic phenomena allows us to access higher levels of consciousness.

In developing our mystical or intuitive abilities, we are opening up our direct hotline to the God force. The tools to do so are all free and simple to use; we require no dependence on outside sources to receive our answers and growth.

There is No Death

Important to the mystical understanding is the realization that there is no death. As we go to sleep at night and dream, our consciousness leaves the physical body and we experience the same place as the death state. Death is merely a transition in our state of awareness. We fear death because we fear the unknown, but we have all died many times.

When we leave the Earth plane it means that the soul has completed its work for this incarnation. For mystics to complete their lessons, its important to identify and release *all* the negative programs. Our goal in graduating from here is to evolve to higher dimensions of learning beyond the Earth. We don't want to have to reincarnate and do a rerun of these negative programs all over again. We are attempting our final incarnation during this lifetime.

At the moment of death, when we cross over, God couldn't care less about your status and material possessions. We will be asked such questions as, "Did you learn to know and love yourself? How did you use and develop the gifts and talents you have within you? What insights and wisdom did you gain? Did you use these gifts to help humankind?"

Our Wake-Up Call

It usually is a dramatic time of change in people's lives that leads them to the spiritual quest. It can be a near-death experience, the loss of a loved one, an illness, a divorce, or any event that knocks a hole in our self-defense wall. In my own case, I had a near-death experience at age thirty-two which changed my beliefs and showed me that I had no idea of my life's true purpose. I had been raised as a fundamentalist Baptist who was told that when you die you are put in the ground and remain there until Gabriel blows his little horn on the final judgment day.

Imagine my surprise as I ascended up and out of my body, which was sick with pneumonia, and saw that I still existed in another dimension. A wise voice told me that this was the death state. It was very a beautiful and peaceful feeling. I could choose to stay there or—if I wanted to go back to my earthly body—obtain an antibiotic within twenty-four hours so that I would not literally die. After seeing the faces of my four children flash by me and seeing my young eighteen-month-old son, I chose to return to my body and get the antibiotic. I realized that I couldn't leave him at this young age.

In seeing there was no death, I realized I better figure out what my life was all about. I knew then I wasn't here just to raise a family and tend to my career. My belief systems were shattered, and my life forever changed. Having this near-death experience also helped me later on in my life when two of my sons were killed. I knew they had gone on to a beautiful place.

People try to keep busy with their work and daily duties to avoid self-responsibility. For people who have had accidents and had to lie in a hospital, this may be the first time in their life they are unable to keep busy and hide from what's truly happening in their lives. They now start to ask, "What is my life all about? Who am I? What is my life? What is my purpose? What am I doing here?"

Powerful events like these are all God's spiritual wake-up calls. Some people will heed the call and others will wait for still another life event to shock them out of their old patterns. Some people are lucky enough to find the spiritual path an easier way—but even this opportunity has been earned from past life experiences. They are now able to pick up the teachings again from their studies in a previous incarnation.

Rewards of the Inner Journey

Developing our mystical gifts puts us in constant contact with the God force, energy, and insight. We find ourselves developing a growing sense of serenity that enables us to be free from anxieties, frustrations, and hostilities. We are more tuned in to ourselves, which allows us to become more in tune with others. The mystery of life reveals itself to us on a daily basis, producing a sense of childlike wonder that celebrates the magic of living. Our communication skills improve significantly, since we can identify our needs and desires, and our focus is clearer. People and situations that used to cause major stress and tension in our lives become less threatening and easier to handle.

We develop an infinite sense of understanding others by focusing more on the real meaning and value of life. Our minds become clearer and our health improves. Although the changes don't always happen overnight and the road at times may seem challenging, opportunities and greater knowledge are always revealed as we delve into the inner self for understanding.

In time, we become very different people than when we first started the spiritual journey. Actualizing our goals becomes the norm and we begin to achieve success on inner and outer levels. Life appears each day as a blank canvas does to an artist. "What am I going to paint today? What do I want to create?"

The co-creator with the divine can create joy, happiness, contentment, adventure, and serenity—certainly not the worry, stress, chaos, and confusion we used to feel when we were powerless victims of life. We can stay centered in the calm eye of the hurricane while the world spins frantically around us.

By clearing out the cobwebs of our own negative programs we are free to enjoy life more. We have much more energy to discover all the beautiful creative gifts, talents, and abilities that God gave us. We see how we create whatever we desire.

This incredible view also provides a tremendous ability to see the humor in all situations. We learn to laugh at our own reactions, which brings us a greater amount of happiness and joy so that we experience life to its fullest. Our journey gets easier and easier as we unload the weight of our fears. The world becomes a supportive rather than a hostile environment.

If we do complete our lessons during this life and are able to stay balanced in body, mind, and spirit, the rewards are immense. We never need to incarnate again on Earth unless we choose to come back into a life of service. We earn the right to be on the celestial level, the plane of the spiritual Masters, when we cross over at death. We can then study with the greatest mystics who have ever walked on the Earth and help our planet from the other side. After so many lifetimes of work, our souls will feel tremendous relief and freedom in completing the Earth journey.

Key Mystical Tools

The force of inner truth depends chiefly on inner stability and preparedness. From this state of mind springs the correct attitude toward the outer world.

—I Ching

In the next six chapters we will explore how life is a learning game. It is our workshop, our laboratory of self-discovery. What is most important in our lifetime is to know ourselves. All experiences, people, and events are there to help us in this process of self-discovery. You'll begin to see that what we perceive as "problems" are always disguised "self-awareness" lessons.

We need to recognize that change first begins within and then the outer reality will follow. We need to center ourselves and raise our energy levels so that we will more clearly perceive what beliefs and attitudes need to change in order for us to fully accept our own divinity. We must learn to listen within to our inner voice and recognize our fears. Then, we can release old patterns, judgments, and limitations and begin to accept and receive our highest good.

Our first tool is MEDITATION:

I ask that for the next six weeks (and hopefully your lifetime!), you will commit to doing the following daily meditation technique. This will heighten your awareness, accelerate your growth, and provide you with a wonderful daily energy boost. To replenish body, mind, and spirit, there is no substitute for meditation.

Daily meditation is our freeway to enlightenment. It opens us to higher energy sources and recharges our energy fields. Our perception depends upon our energy level, and meditation is the way to keep energy at its highest. It gives us the eyes to see and the ears to hear how we are creating our lives. The more we meditate daily, the more we can hear our inner voice.

Although some positive changes are experienced immediately from meditating, many are gradual. Besides a reduction in stress and tension, an overall improvement in health and feelings of peacefulness are common. You'll discover an inner reservoir of strength and well-being as you attune to your spiritual center.

With daily meditation we can pack in twenty years' worth of lessons in one year's time. This is because we're taking positive actions and giving less energy to the fears, anxieties, tensions, and stress that keep us separate from God. Life goes much smoother and faster when we get out of our own way.

Life becomes a game, a fun, exciting adventure. We will find the little things that once disturbed us disappearing after several months of daily meditation. After a couple of years, the big things stop bothering us. We will find that we don't react to situations and people as we did previously.

Once we accustom ourselves to sitting for the twenty-minute period, we'll look forward eagerly to each session. It is best to meditate when we are alert, rather than after a big meal or when we are very tired. You may find the morning hours best, so that you can heighten your energy and orient in a positive way before beginning each day. Or, you may rather meditate right before going to sleep. This will help you clear out the clutter from the day and raise your energy so that you are more receptive to the teaching dreams that come at night.

Choose a time which best suits your personal schedule. Despite how busy or full your schedule might be, always make time for your meditation. To me, it is as important as food and sleep to maintain a healthy existence. You should choose a time when it is quiet and you will not be disturbed, as loud noises can be jolting in the middle of meditation.

How to Meditate

This method of meditation is simple but powerful. It should be done on a daily basis for twenty minutes. The easiest way to meditate is to listen to your favorite songs and music, keeping your mind gently focused on the music.

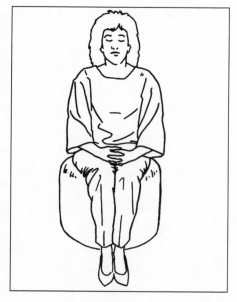

Figure 1

1. Sit in a chair with your spine erect, shoulders relaxed, and feet flat on the floor. Fold your hands together in your lap and close your eyes. (See figure 1.)

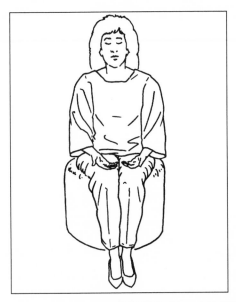

Figure 2

2. Take three slow, deep breaths, exhaling to the base of your spine, and feel yourself relaxing. Sit with your hands together for ten minutes.

3. After ten minutes, open your hands, palms up, laying them gently in your lap. (See figure 2.) Keep your focus on the songs and if your mind strays, gently bring it back to the music.

4. At the end of the twenty minutes, close your hands into fists and feel a balloon of white light a city block around, above, and underneath you so that you're in the center. (See figure 3.) This sends love and healing out to the masses and buffers stress and negativity from coming back into you. This "closing down" technique protects your energy field.

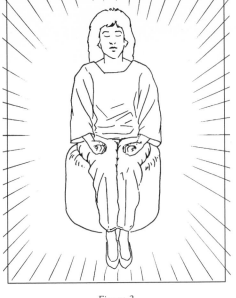

Figure 3

It takes most people at least twenty years to still the mind, so we should not be discouraged if our minds wander while we meditate. The ability to focus grows each day. This twenty-minute period, however, is not our only practice. We should also endeavor to practice the meditative attitude, watching our thoughts and behavior throughout each day. Meditation can thus help us to be more fully involved in life because we can watch how we program our life experiences by our thoughts, words, and beliefs about ourselves. Sometimes the changes are dramatic and sometimes they are subtle. But meditation does change our lives because it changes us.

This meditation technique is perfectly suited for the high-speed world in which we live. Until quite recently, people were usually not given the mystical teachings unless they were living in monasteries or ashrams. Other techniques of meditation can open the five senses and bring in the sixth sense or intuitive abilities. But, if we're not living in a monastery or ashram, we need the closing down at the end of the meditation to protect our energy and mystical gifts. Otherwise, as we go out into the world, the energy we've awakened during meditation will be drained from us.

Our second tool is our DREAMS:

We spend ten days of every month in the sleep state—which is a third of our lives we're missing if we're not working with our dreams. Our dreams provide a door to the divine mind for answers and higher teachings to help us in our daily lives. They play a vital part in developing spiritual awareness.

Dreams may occur on many levels. We all leave the body at night to receive higher teachings. Dreams are how our Guidance can show us when we are going off the track in our lessons and what needs to be corrected. As we interpret the symbols and story line in our dream, we will find insight into our daily lives. We also receive praise and acknowledgment in dreams when we are doing a great job.

Everyone and everything in a dream represents some aspect of us. People in the dream usually represent the qualities within ourselves we have projected onto others. Male figures represent our strong, assertive part. Females represent our sensitive, intuitive, feminine side. We each possess both male and female aspects.

A child in a dream represents our child part. An aged person is an old part of ourselves, either one that is wise or one that is dying because we have outgrown it. Animals represent feelings or characteristics that we associate with them.

A house, building, or store is us. If it is large, it indicates our great potential and awareness of opportunities. Any vehicle symbolizes how we are traveling through our everyday lives. Going uphill shows we're headed the right direction. Downhill, backwards, or out of control says we're going in the wrong direction and need to re-direct our energies.

Water shows us how our emotional states are doing. Nightmares are there to show us our fears. Everything has a significance. Working with dreams is like learning a new language and understanding our lives from a wonderfully detached and wise perspective. All dreams are positive once we work out their symbology.

Keep a daily dream journal while taking this course and record all dreams. We will list one dream each week in our worksheets. If we don't remember our dreams, we can program our minds nightly to get a recall. Sit on the side of the bed, take three slow deep breaths and say, "I *will* have a dream tonight. I *will* wake up and remember the dream. I *will* write the dream down." Keep the journal on your nightstand and record each dream immediately following it.

The daily meditation will also help us to have the energy to recall a dream. Our dreams are priceless messages from our Guidance on identifying and resolving the problem areas which block us from our true success, love, and abundance. For this course and a lifetime of help, I highly recommend my book, *The Dream Book: Symbols for Self-Understanding*. It offers easy instructions for using and interpreting dreams and their symbology. It contains over 1600 dream symbols and their meanings. People from all over the world have found it accurate and simple to use.

Our third tool is AFFIRMATIONS AND VISUALIZATIONS:

We are unlimited beings who have been programmed to be limited. Our lives are a reflection of what we think we deserve. Affirmations and visualizations are prayers that use our creative powers to manifest what we want in life. The mind is like a computer and responds to whatever we program it to receive. The Bible said, "Ask and you shall receive," but it should have added, "If you don't ask, you don't get!" We have to develop enough self-love and esteem to know we deserve to receive the prosperity we seek.

God has given each of us the creative power to manifest whatever we want in life. We already have all the richness and love of the divine spirit within us. When we affirm and feel love and wholeness, we will bring it into our lives. If we affirm prosperity, we invite it to dwell in our consciousness and lifestyle.

Most of us ask for things out of a feeling of lack or separateness; rather, we should acknowledge our oneness with God and our divine birthright as spiritual beings. If we surround our prayers with feelings of doubt, unworthiness, and worry we can undermine our own efforts.

Also, throughout the day, when we hear our negative thinking, mentally say, "Cancel, Cancel," then program in a positive message. For example if we hear ourselves saying, "I sure am getting fat," say, "Cancel, Cancel," and then say, "I am losing weight easily." We may have to cancel thoughts fifty times a day the first few months! This is a very powerful mystical tool of transformation.

Thoughts are very powerful. Even lightly stated negative comments are recorded by the mind and will reflect back on us. Many of us dismiss any positive input from ourselves or others. In receiving a compliment such as, "You sure look beautiful today in that dress," we may be inclined to respond, "Oh, this old thing has been hanging in my closet for years." Learn to take in loving remarks and smile and just say thank you. Likewise, we should not be afraid to express love and appreciative remarks to those around us.

We must fill ourselves with a strong sense of love, power, and connection to God with our statements. Feel and say each affirmation three times assertively. An example would be, "The perfect career is manifesting in my life now. Every day I awaken with joy and unlimited energy." We can devise an affirmation for whatever we are choosing to create, such as the perfect partner, house, job, knowledge, direction. The best time to practice daily affirmations is at the end of our meditation before the closing down process when we close our hands into a fist. We can do as many affirmations as we like. Visualizing our goals and putting great feeling and joy into them makes it easier to attract what we desire.

Scientific research has shown that we're using only one sixth of our brain cells. The rest of them aren't there just for stuffing! By developing our mystical gifts we are waking up the brain cells that now lie dormant. We are each composed of electromagnetic energy. When we meditate, we are charging these cells to re-awaken them. This re-awakening develops our brain power and capacity to create. There are no limits except the ones we impose upon ourselves.

Included in each of the weekly lessons in this book will be a *Guided Visualization* exercise. These imagery exercises will help us to gain a deeper understanding of our life experiences. We'll imagine ourselves in different scenarios talking to our relationships, our teachers, or our inner child, or facing a problem that needs guidance. We will record our insights from these sessions.

Lesson of the Week

Besides using the tools of Meditation, Dreams, and Affirmations and Visualizations and doing the weekly exercises, please fill in the *Lesson of the Week* question in each week's worksheets. Each week, write in at least one positive lesson you learned. For greater self-insight, you can also keep a daily journal of your "lesson of the day" if you like.

As we watch our fears and old programs emerge throughout our day, we can imagine ourselves as a newspaper reporter, sitting in a comfy chair in our "third eye" center. This center is known as the one eye of truth located between the eyebrows. It is where we can observe all our reactions and see life from a wise, detached, non-judgmental position. We can perceive events in our lives from God's or our Guidance's point of view—as teaching lessons that can enhance the quality of our lives. (We'll talk more about this and other energy centers in Week 4.)

Contrary to popular belief, even mistakes and fears all have positive messages for us. For instance, we often learn the importance of verbalizing our needs to others by seeing the results when we don't communicate. When we lose our energy, forget to take care of our needs, become critical of ourselves and others, say *yes* when we mean *no*, we are taught about making wiser choices in the future.

We will record in the workbook where we reacted and how we might better respond next time to the situation. We can also write down instances where we didn't react, and where we verbalized our needs well. We're taking notes and doing research in studying these amazing creatures—ourselves!

When you react to a situation, ask yourself:

1. How did I set it up? (What patterns am I creating that this situation is bringing up to show me?)
2. What is my positive lesson?
3. What can I do to change and heal the situation?

Then you can picture how you would like to handle the situation.

This self-questioning is a great training tool for understanding what areas in our lives need some help and guidance. We'll find that we have much more time for creating all the wonderful, positive things we want as we take self-responsibility.

Every day is a new classroom for learning. We will study the results of our thoughts, words, and actions and see how they affect our reality.

Ordinary People for an Extraordinary Quest

Living a mystical life is an opportunity that is available to everyone. This spiritual practice is not just for special individuals. Each of us is a unique and equal child of God who can tap into the divine force throughout his or her life. Jesus, who was the greatest mystic of all time, said, "The works that I do you shall do also; and greater works than these shall you do." He was showing us how we all possess this divine connection and can use it to create great acts of love just as he did.

The teachings provided here are very simple and easy to use. In this time of great transformation on the Earth, we need as many people as possible developing their spirituality and intuitive abilities to help produce a change within the self and our world.

We will each respond in our own unique way on this journey. We will effect change upon everyone around us, whether we choose to function as teachers of the masses or to maintain our ordinary lifestyle in our communities. We may choose to express our divine nature quietly within, or overtly through writing, lecturing, art, music, film, politics, business, or the healing professions.

This mystical work doesn't require any previous spiritual training. What is necessary is the zest and desire to face our fears and accept total responsibility for our life experiences.

I did not have any knowledge of meditation or metaphysics before I began to explore the mystical teachings. I was a housewife with four children and hadn't even heard the word "psychic" before. Then in 1967, two years after my near-death experience, I connected with my Guidance and began channeling these teachings. I was told that I would be a teacher of teachers and that I had to live everything I was taught before I could receive any further mystical training. I began to see how others were responsible for setting up their life situations and figured that I must be doing the same thing. This process took many years of self-discovery work and I've been able to help many others develop their own spiritual abilities through offering the seeds of self-growth.

We're in a make-it-or-break-it transition time on our planet. We, as a species, are going either to return to our spiritual values and balance our priorities to improve world conditions, or once again destroy our civilization through power, greed, and corruption. The choice is ours and the work begins within the self.

Assignment for Week 2:

- *Do* your daily twenty-minute meditation.

- *Write* down any dreams you have this week.

- *Practice* daily affirmations and visualizations.

- *Read* Week 2, and fill out the "Getting to Know You" worksheets.

Week 2

SELF-LOVE:
Dare to Be You!

Whatever you can do or dream you can, begin it. Boldness has genius, magic and power in it. Begin it now.

—Goethe

There is only one person who needs to give us permission to be ourselves—that person is us. What we are—our unique blend of strengths, talents, and abilities—is unmatched anywhere in the universe. To fully activate these abilities and give ourselves the time and freedom to do so is our biggest life challenge.

How we respond to life is the whole secret of happiness and success. Feeling afraid, paralyzed in self-doubt, and worrying about what people will think of us will get us nowhere. We will miss our opportunity for growth.

Self-love and self-esteem should not come from what we do but from who we are. They are within. No one out there can give us self-worth, value, or security. They must come from inside ourselves.

The message of karma is to learn to love ourselves. As we fully love and honor the God within our own being, we fully love and honor the God within all beings. We can then never hurt self or another soul.

All of our lessons evolve around self-love. To love self we must go beyond ego identification and attachments. The true self is the spiritual energy within, the creative power behind all forms. Love is the absence of fear, and fear is the last great illusion that separates us from inner truth.

We are free to create our own heaven or hell on Earth. It is just as easy and a lot more fun to create our own personal paradise to share with others.

Understanding Our Life Purpose

The mystical teachings can provide us with a complete understanding about the nature and purpose of our life's journey. The mystic's way explains why we had to go through such challenging situations and relationships and how they were all necessary for us to become who we are today.

We begin to look underneath the life story and see it as a great mirror of opportunity to grow. Through meditation and self-observation we are able to see the roles that people have played in our lives. We see how everyone has been an actor in our play, reflecting our inner life and self-awareness beliefs. Even the people who played the "bad guy" roles turn out to be some of our greatest teachers.

Through this perception, we can achieve a higher level of detachment and trust so that we are not over-reacting emotionally to others. We are all setting up our lessons for what needs to be learned. It is no longer our job to correct other people's problems. The focus is on our self-growth work.

The mystic realizes that no source outside the self is needed in order to grow. While friends, groups, programs, and teachers may help us on our journey, tapping the wellspring of answers and self-development is solely an inner process. The entire world is our teacher and we are free to learn and grow whether we are alone or with the masses. No one else's behavior needs to impact upon our growth unless we choose to allow them to do so.

Our way in life may not follow the traditional routes that others have taken. We need to be patient with ourselves and listen to our own inner voice to guide us through our life's journey. It is important not to give ourselves negative suggestions about finding our purpose in life. Rather than saying, "I'm confused and I don't know what my purpose is," we can say to ourselves, "My life purpose is getting clearer and clearer. I'm being led to my perfect work and goals in God's perfect way."

Self-Love in Today's World

By meditating and putting our light out there, we become a beacon to the world. It takes only one positive person to change the energy of one thousand negative people. If we are willing to put in the time, effort, and energy to be aware, to face and confront our fears and walk through them, we will become loving examples of this process to our families, friends, communities, and the world. The world is in transition with its crises of economics, government corruption, racism, sexism and the environment. We can effect change in the world and those around us.

People are affected by our light. We teach by our example. In loving deeply we help inspire others to develop their creative and spiritual potential. We are pioneers in a field that has long been forgotten by humankind. In the past, the mystical secrets were hidden from the masses. The time has come to bring forth these teachings to show how love does triumph over our fears and negative patterns. Jesus said that the Kingdom of Heaven is within, and if we go within we'll know God. What he meant was: Be still and listen! The answers to any problem lie within us. My Guidance has said:

"Life is school. You should be constantly growing, constantly changing and excited about the changes, for they are not negative changes. You are all so frightened of change. Why does change bother you? Change means expansion. If you stay in your own limited realm, how can you grow? What will you know?

"You may have to clean up negative things in order to advance, but it's the same as when you were a child and had some lessons to pass in the first grade before going on to the second grade. How does this differ? It differs by the importance you place on it and what you think of yourself.

"Most people in our society measure themselves by the university degrees that they have, the jobs they perform, the car they drive, or the home that they own. These things mean nothing to God. The only thing that means anything when you leave the Earth plane is how well you developed your inner potential and how well you used your talents and abilities. These are the things that are important for self-exploration.

"You go in without clothes; you leave without same. The only things that you have gathered are the tools, the knowledge, the techniques that you have learned while you were there. These are important. To not try to make an effort to better yourself and your conditions is saying you have given up on yourself.

"It is the same as if you stayed in the first grade as a child—as if you didn't bother to do the homework and make the necessary changes to get into the second grade. You may complain about it; you may not like it, and that's acceptable. We understand your complaining, but go on.

"As a child you would never think of giving up. So don't stop now. Continue growing and learning. It doesn't end with college. It doesn't end at thirty. It doesn't end at forty, fifty, sixty. Life is eternal. These are eternal lessons. The excitement comes each day. Live one day at a time. See what gifts are presented to you through watching others, through seeing your own reactions to things and situations, and deal with those.

"This will keep you busy for your whole life. People are always looking for something more stimulating. The problem in the world today is too many people are looking outside themselves. Truth is not out there someplace. Truth lies within."

Balance vs. Perfection

The difference between trying to become balanced and trying to be perfect is that we can succeed at the first task. We can never succeed at the second. We are not here to learn to be perfect. We are here to learn to balance our masculine, feminine, adult, child, and other aspects of self.

Each of us is here to learn to know ourselves, and it is for this reason that we are going to make mistakes, we are going to have to re-do lessons. It is important to understand that it is in making errors, wrong judgments, and decisions for ourselves that we really learn. If we can do them joyously with a sense of humor, we can make this incarnation a joyful experience filled with adventure. We shouldn't take ourselves so seriously.

Every situation that occurs is truly positive. Each situation may seem negative while we are experiencing it, but it is an opportunity for growth and learning. We learn which pathways to follow in order to achieve our goals. As Shakespeare said, "All the world's a stage, And all the men and women merely players; They have their exits and their entrances; And one man in his time plays many parts."

Actually, all of our negative programs stem from an inability to really love the self. Because we do not see ourselves for what we really are, we become afraid, insecure, and a host of other negatives that all reflect our personal fears. The true self is spirit, light, and energy. The self can take on thousands of forms, wear hundreds of different hats, play many different roles. Our essence lies underneath all the forms and thoughts.

We all possess both the strong, assertive masculine aspects as well as the sensitive, intuitive parts of self. Our roles and choices as men and women are shifting to include all possibilities in partnerships and careers. In identifying ourselves only as someone's spouse, lover, employee, relative, or friend, we limit our awareness and manifestation of our infinite potential.

One of the best and fastest ways to succeed at developing our potential and knowing ourselves is through meditating. In keeping our energy up and recharged on a daily basis we are able to perceive and release the old ideas and blocks that have limited us. We connect with the very core of our beings, our God Self, which infinitely loves us, lives in us, breathes us and guides us. This gives us self-confidence in our abilities to create. For if we are given an aspiration, we are also given the power and means to carry it out.

The purpose of each individual's unfoldment is to go within the self, to find one's own truth and answers. When we love and value ourselves, we send out a message to others that we deserve love. If we send out the vibration of "I'm not worthy, or come dump here," people will reflect this back to us.

Changing Aloneness into All-Oneness

When we feel alone or apart, we see ourselves as victims, strangers to this world, unloved and unappreciated. We forget that we have created our life story, and that we are free to change it at any moment. We have forgotten who we really are—the creative, unifying energy, the God force behind all appearances. This separation leads to low energy, self-pitying thoughts, lack of self-nurturing, and a lack of trust of self and others.

We must constantly practice connecting with the true self. When we become attached to things or experiences, we lose touch with the energy that created them in the first place. Our universe is abundant and we can choose to create any new situation or environment when we allow ourselves to remember our power and oneness with God.

In this way, we realize that we are never alone, but are always "all one" with this love energy. Feeling connected to the God force allows us to be at peace and happy with our lives. We accept ourselves as we are and can love others unconditionally as well. We feel empowered to create and choose whatever we want in life. It is a feeling of great freedom and liberation.

Need for Appreciation

We often hear the statement: "You have to love yourself before anyone else can love you." The reason this is true is that when we love ourselves, we send out a vibration to others that we are worthy of love, of being loved. If we don't love ourselves, a vibration of "I'm not worthy" goes out and we draw others to us who are not capable of loving either themselves or us. We are all vibrating what we really feel on an unseen level all the time.

If we want to be loved more, we must first begin to love, appreciate, and value ourselves. This will change our vibrations to attract more love to us. If we realize that God loves us just as we are, how can we do any less? We need to take stock of all the positive qualities and characteristics we possess and focus on them. We can reinforce our unique and lovable nature.

Dare to Be You!

You are the only person that needs to give yourself permission to be yourself. Of all the billions of people ever created, there is no one else with your specific combination of talents, gifts, and abilities. To fully activate these abilities is your greatest opportunity and challenge in life. Celebrate yourself!

By fearing to follow our dreams or worrying about being accepted by others, we miss our whole life's adventures. We have to really *desire* to be free to develop our true divine selves. We cannot allow ourselves to be victimized by anyone or anything. We always have a choice to respond to any situation in a new, positive, uplifted state. The mystic transforms the old patterns into the new ways, the darkness into the light.

Here are some other useful guidelines that help us to make decisions and strengthen our self-growth journey:

Walking Your Own Path and Finding Your Own Truth

1. The truth of your own being is stronger than any experience, thing, idea, or belief. Boldly tell the truth to yourself.

2. Choose to grow into full self-awareness. Desire it more than anything.

3. Do not submit your integrity to anyone or anything. Honor your dignity in all situations and with all people.

4. Be willing to make and take responsibility for all your own decisions and choices. No one else can make your decisions for you.

5. A simple rule of thumb: Say "yes" to whatever uplifts you, strengthens your sense of self, and moves you forward; say "no" to whatever dissipates your energy, holds you back, or goes against your intuition.

6. Only when you place yourself first can you establish genuine relationships with others.

7. Only when nurturing your personal integrity and following your own life path will you maintain optimum mental, emotional, and physical health.

8. Your strength of independence and purpose will be an inspiration to others to grow and develop their own awareness. This is the greatest gift you can give to self and others.

■ *Getting to Know You* Worksheets

I. Reflect on your daily meditation practice this week. What has been your experience? Did you do it daily? Did you have problems in meditation?

_____

_____

_____

_____

_____

_____

As you begin meditating and your growth starts to accelerate, you may have some of the following experiences: tingling sensations in your hands, rushes of energy up the spine, a gentle back-and-forth rocking motion. These are all normal occurrences.

As the energy moves up the spine, it releases the blocks in your body. If it feels like the energy is stuck or constricted in an area, just visualize the energy moving up through the body, out the top of the head, and going up to the sun.

If the energy ever feels too intense while you're meditating, close one finger and thumb in each hand. Remember you are always in control and there is nothing to fear.

II. How did you do with remembering your dreams this week? Describe a dream you had and what message you received from it.

_____

_____

_____

_____

_____

III. What was your experience in using affirmations and visualizations this week? Which ones have you chosen to use?

_____

_____

_____

_____

_____

Self-Love Affirmation: "I have all the love and power within me now."

IV. Lesson of the Week

Write down at least one positive thing you learned during the past week. Review where you reacted and look to discover a new way to respond as a self-empowered, loving being:

_____

_____

_____

_____

_____

_____

V. The inner teacher of wisdom and knowledge is always there to radiate light through our momentary programs and illusions. It's this inner light, shining through the images and beliefs, that gives true insight. You are entrusted with priceless talents, gifts, and abilities for creating a joyous world. Reflect on the following words and complete the statements with what seems most true for you at this time:

1. My most valuable talents and abilities are:

_____

_____

_____

2. Talents or abilities I don't think I have but would truly like to develop are:

_____

_____

_____

3. I can be true to myself in this lifetime by:

_____

_____

_____

4. The most positive qualities I like about myself and others are:

_____

_____

_____

5. The most negative things I sometimes think or say about myself or others are:

_____

_____

_____

6. The most important limiting belief I would like to give up about myself is:

_____

_____

_____

7. Meditation and self-growth to me mean:

_____

_____

_____

8. My basic philosophy of life is:

_____

_____

_____

_____

It is important to know yourself so you are able to communicate your needs and feelings to yourself and others. This is the self-love process. We tend to blame others or situations for not meeting our needs when our most common mistake has been that we have not clearly defined and communicated what we want.

VI. Imagine that it is far in the future and you have just finished all your lessons in this life and crossed over to the other side. Congratulate yourself on doing such a fantastic job while you were on Earth.

Now see yourself picking up a copy of a major daily newspaper and on the front page is a picture of you and news of your death. They also published a eulogy in your honor, listing all you accomplished for yourself and the world. Write what was said:

_____

_____

_____

_____

Reflect on your words. Was it difficult to come up with a list of your positive attributes and achievements? Did you discover it was important to list the inner goals attained (such as wisdom, balance, serenity, patience) as well as the outer goals? The more you believe in yourself and your ability to create these qualities, the more you will attract your own success.

1. List two situations in your life right now that seem limiting or upsetting and that you'd like to change (relationships, job, health etc.):

_____

_____

_____

_____

2. Now, sitting quietly in a meditative position with eyes closed, take three slow, deep breaths and turn your palms up. Picture or feel a very wise teacher sitting opposite you. Ask this teacher, "What are the key ways I can help to resolve these problems?" Listen deeply for the answers. Use your imagination to get the conversation going and just let it flow. Write down any thoughts you hear:

_____

_____

_____

_____

_____

This is an exercise you can use at the end of your meditation whenever you get stuck with a problem or issue. If you have trouble hearing an answer, just relax and listen deeply. Your imagination is the bridge to God consciousness. If you try too hard you're going to block the insights from coming. Relax the intellect and play with the exercises as a child would play a game.

VII. One way to get in touch with your programs is to make a list of some the adjectives you use to describe yourself, both positively and negatively. List eight of these here:

1._____

2._____

3._____

4._____

5._____

6._____

7._____

8._____

Circle the numbers that say something negative about yourself. Now create a positive affirmation to replace this program. For example, if you listed that you are "confused and stuck," change it to "I am flexible and open to learning." Or, if you put "overweight," you can now program, "I'm beautiful and my body weight is adjusting to its happiest form." List your new affirmations next to the negative adjectives above.

When you hear these negative thoughts in your head, remember to say, "Cancel, Cancel" and mentally replace them with the positive affirmations. Your thoughts are very powerful and determine how your life will be. If you want to increase your self-esteem, you have to work from within yourself, love yourself, and know you deserve love and success. The universe is already unlimited and prosperous. It is your divine right to claim this abundance.

VIII. Guided Visualization

Working with guided imagery in our visualizations is a means of tapping into a higher power or source that exists within. We create through the right brain. Using our imaginations is the key to receiving insight from God, our Guidance, and our Higher Self. All wisdom and knowledge await us. Learning how to tap into this force is what we're going to be doing through working with the exercises each week.

The mind is like a computer: what it produces depends on how we program it. So if we have fears, guilts, or shames that we're putting in, this is exactly what we're going to draw into our lives. By clearing out old patterns and getting answers for problems in our lives, guided visualizations enable us to perceive situations from a much deeper level.

Whatever we correct within ourselves is going to change the outer reality. We can't change our outer life unless we change it from within. We can heal and understand our relationships and challenging situations from a higher perspective. The visualization exercises can have profound impact on our life experiences.

To achieve the best results from these exercises, I recommend that each week you make a cassette tape of each guided visualization in your own voice. You can have soft, relaxing music playing in the background if you like. Take a pause wherever you see ". . ." You can use male or female pronouns in the exercise depending on what's appropriate. For simplification, I have used male pronouns.

Listen to the guided visualization exercise while sitting in a meditative position with your eyes closed, palms up in your lap. Start by focusing on your breathing and letting go of all the stress tension in your body. After the exercise, write down any insights, realizations and gifts you received.

I want to first do an exercise to show you how easy and simple it is to use guided visualizations. People sometimes say, "I can't see anything," when they first try the exercises. *Feel* it if you can't see it.

So, to begin with, relax, and take three slow, deep breaths . . .
Now imagine yourself walking up to your front door . . .
You have your keys in your hand . . . How many keys are on your keychain? . . . What does your keychain look like? . . . What does your door key look like? . . . Now imagine yourself standing at the door, and you're putting the key in the lock. . . . What does the door look like? . . . Does it need to be painted? . . . Does it have any scratches on it? . . . Now turn the door handle, open the door, and as you open the

door, what's the first thing you see as you walk into your
house? . . . Now as you walk in, I want you to go into the
kitchen, and on the kitchen counter is an apple. Pick up this
apple and feel it. . . . What does the apple feel like? . . .
What color is the apple? . . . Does it have a stem? . . . Now
set the apple down and pick up a peach. . . . What does the
peach feel like? . . . What color is the peach? . . . Now set
the peach down, and pick up an avocado. . . . What does the
avocado feel like? Is it ripe, or is it hard? . . . Now set the
avocado down, . . . and open your eyes.

Visualizing isn't really a new skill. We do it all day long. When we
get in the car and we take off to wherever we're going, we don't always
stop to think how we're getting there. The imagination just creates and
we go. So what we're learning to do is to dial in, as if to a frequency
for a radio station, to the knowledge we are seeking. Whatever we
want, we can tune into that.

There is no time or space between us and the source, so we are
always free to tap into this inner source. Whether we call it God, our
Guidance, or Higher Self, it's an inner source that all of us possess. All
creative ideas come from this source. Here's a visualization exercise to
meet a wise teacher:

Imagine yourself at the beach . . . It's a beautiful summer
day. You're sitting on a blanket and hear the ocean waves
softly crashing in the background . . . Feel the warm breeze
blowing on your face and through your hair . . . Your toes
are digging into the soft warm sand . . . As you look up into
the sky, you see a bright ball of light coming down towards
you . . . It lands right in front of you and in the light you see
a wise Master teacher, who is here to help you with anything

you wish to know . . . This teacher loves you far more than you have ever been loved before. . . . He extends his arms towards you and gives you a big hug . . . Feel the powerful golden light of his energy field surrounding you . . . You melt in his presence.

The teacher now points to a cave near the beach you hadn't seen before . . . Out of the cave, you see a delightful, bouncy child coming towards you . . . It is you at age five . . . The child comes up to you and you embrace him as he climbs up into your lap . . . Now ask him, "What do you need from me now to help make our life happier?" . . . Pause and listen deeply for the child's reply . . . When he is done, the child jumps off your lap . . . Thank the child for his ideas and promise him that you will make time for them.

Next you see a fifteen-year-old boy coming out of the cave and walking towards you . . . It's you as a teenager . . . Hug the teenager and ask him, "What do you need from me now to help make our life happier?" . . . Listen to his response . . . Thank the teenager for his help.

Now you see a final figure coming from the cave . . . It's a wise, elderly person . . . This is you at the end of your life's journey . . . He is full of light and knowledge . . . Hug this person and ask, "What do you need from me now to help make our life happier?" . . . Listen for the reply.

Now thank all three parts of you for coming to help you on your journey . . . You will do your best to follow their advice.

The teacher disappears with the three of them up into the sky in a ball of light . . . You wave good-bye . . . Now feel yourself lifting off the sand and coming back into your body and this room.

Slowly open your eyes and write down what insights you received during this exercise:

_____

_____

_____

_____

_____

_____

_____

IX. Assignment for Week 3:

- *Do* your daily twenty-minute meditation.

- *Write* down any dreams you have this week.

- *Practice* daily affirmations and visualizations.

- *Read* Week 3, and fill out the "Cleaning Out Negative Baggage" worksheets.

Week 3

RELEASING THE PAST AND FACING FEARS

There is but one cause of human failure and that is man's lack of faith in his true Self.

—William James

Impact of Past Patterns

In order to find enjoyment, energy, and freedom today, it is important that we develop the ability to overcome guilt, shame, and remorse about our past. We need to identify the positive lesson behind our life experiences, then forgive ourselves and others for the choices made.

In learning to transform our negative patterns into positive ones, we first have to honestly examine them. We identify these patterns and release the ones we no longer wish to keep. Otherwise, we experience suffering in our lives because of our limited beliefs that we are victims of circumstance.

Our universe is abundant and our creative energy is unlimited. What we are really attempting to do is to break out of these limiting beliefs. Gradually, layer by layer, we must eliminate all the old programs that stand in the way of knowing our divine potential. We can then use our free will to create lives of growth and fulfillment, once we understand how to direct our energy towards our positive goals.

It is important to remember that we chose whatever people or situations we encountered in our early years. We selected the people and lessons of our first twenty-eight years very carefully, prior to incarnating. These relationships were wisely selected in order to advance our souls in clearing up the unhealed energies of our past. We didn't choose the difficult ones just to suffer. It was part of our lessons to learn about ourselves. We also set up these experiences to release karma from past lives. Karma refers to the law or principle which governs one's experiences over collective lifetimes and within the individual lifetime. Some people call it the law of cause and effect, and it simply means that we will harvest exactly what we have planted. It is the principle of individual responsibility: we control our own destiny by our thoughts, words and deeds. These challenging circumstances can be turned into opportunities to gain great wisdom, compassion, and self-understanding. Also, we may have chosen extremely difficult lessons so that later we could teach others on the subject.

Our negative attitudes, habits, and thought patterns block the flow of energy throughout our beings, create stress, limit our perspective, and immobilize our actions with fear. Releasing ourselves from fear, anxiety, and guilt is a prerequisite to gaining fuller control of mental, emotional, physical, and spiritual processes. It is necessary to gain confidence in ourselves and in our abilities to trust our intuitive powers. By retraining our minds to develop positive, healthy self-images, we effect the success of our relationships, career, finances, and sense of well-being. Doing this inner work is necessary for mystical development.

Changing habits and attitudes does require work. We have to accept total responsibility for our parts in creating our life scenarios. We'd like to be able to blame others for the way our lives have gone. As mystics, we realize that we have set up others to reflect our negative programs in order for us to see and change these programs *in ourselves*.

The basic message of these old programs is that we are either less than everyone, and have to try constantly to win other people's approval, or that we're greater than everyone, and our job is to shape everyone up to our higher level of consciousness. The "less than, better than" comparison is an endless, hopeless struggle. Both of these stances are based on our insecurities and lack of self-love.

We finally learn to stop, see ourselves as we truly are, access our positive qualities and strengths, own our weaknesses, and work to develop ourselves. This self-acceptance leads to unconditional love for the self and others. The search for it outside ourselves must end.

Many of our role models were very dysfunctional. But in every life experience there was always something positive to be learned and gained. Alcoholic parents show us by example how trying to numb one's painful feelings through substance abuse will never work. A parent who plays a submissive, co-dependent role teaches us how the martyr role never leads to personal happiness and fulfillment. A workaholic or absent parent shows us how the pain of running away from being intimate creates an empty existence as well.

If we review and release these patterns, we no longer have to continue the suffering programs. We are then free to create whatever we want in our lives. Otherwise, we tend to repeat the same avoidance behaviors.

This is the gift of freedom this mystical work offers. We are like a cocoon waiting to unravel the web of old negative patterns surrounding us. In letting go of the patterns, we become like beautiful butterflies soaring zestfully through life. We are no longer victims of our past, our present, or any future situations. Life is full of options and choices.

Our relationship to our bodies improves and our health improves as we let go of these old energies. Our minds become refreshed with new ideas for living and creating joy. Our spirits begin tapping into greater energy and guidance for living a truly loving life. We enjoy feeling and being more alive and intimate in all our relationships.

With daily meditation, we will develop the energy to see each situation from a calm, detached place, rather than taking a reactive position. In each challenging situation, remember to ask: "What was my positive lesson in seeing that? Why would I have gone through that?" If we lived through abusive childhood experiences that we didn't have the power to stop, we can certainly take back our control in situations now so no one can continue to abuse us. That's our responsibility from here on out.

Erasing Childhood Programming

Most of us grew up in families and a society that gave us many limiting programs relating to our emotional development and intuitive abilities. We were told, "Good girls/boys don't cry." We may have been punished verbally or physically if our self-expression wasn't comfortable for our role models. Many of our feelings were invalidated and deemed negative. As a result, we learned to suppress our hurt, anger, and pain. We molded ourselves into what was acceptable to our parents, teachers, peers, community, and society.

It can be extremely useful to examine the beliefs and attitudes of our role models to help us to see if we have identified with their limited patterns. Our natural sense of vulnerability to feel deeper levels of emotions and sensory input may have become stifled. We may have become numb to our feeling states and suppressed our inner voice and intuition. Feeling certain emotions became unacceptable and as a result were hidden away.

Our feelings and emotions are our links to intuition and spiritual awareness. Our emotions are our barometers for keeping the mind, body, and spirit in balance. They are our channels to higher levels of self-consciousness and the awakening of our greater power. We may have suppressed our uncomfortable feelings for so long that we began to think of them as bad, dark, and unspiritual. The truth is that once we open up to the experience of feeling and releasing these denied aspects, we make room for the light and energy to flood the being. It is a feeling of great joy, ecstasy, and insight to open up to the deeper levels of feeling and being.

Besides learning to suppress the emotions, many of us were programmed to believe mental patterns such as, "You're stupid" or "You're ugly" or "You'll never amount to anything." We may have internalized these stifling voices that we heard and that now create our own inner negative critic. This is why it's so important to listen to and review our daily thoughts and remember to cancel out these negative ideas.

Working on reprogramming our beliefs involves affirming new positive programs as we dig in and clean out all the unnecessary baggage we carry. As we take self-responsibility and clean up all the fears and negative programs such as, "I don't deserve love," "I'm not worthy," "I can't, I won't" or "It's impossible," and replace them with positive ones such as, "I deserve the best life has to offer," "The perfect career is manifesting for me now," and "I'm being divinely guided in all that I do," then a whole new world of insight and freedom begins to open up for us. Within a short period of time we are going to have the new positive way of seeing it.

Uncovering Your Fears

While we are on this self-growth journey, it may seem that there are endless fears we have to deal with, but there are really only five or six major ones. Everyone's biggest fears are rejection or abandonment. Others include death, illness, intimacy, failure, and success. These fears manifest in countless ways such as hurt, envy, guilt, jealousy, self-pity, rage, and all the other negative emotions you can name. Fear, in its many guises, is most responsible for creating stress within our bodies and blocking us on our paths to fulfillment.

Fear separates us from loving anyone. There's an old saying, "We can't love God and fear God at the same time." The same is true of all our relationships. Fear blocks us from love. It's important to face and eliminate our fears one by one. If we confront them, knowing that we have the power to choose how we want to react, this will enable us to walk through them so the fear no longer has power over us.

My Guidance has said:

"Recognize that in each situation you always have a choice. You can choose to learn and grow from each lesson or react with fear. There is nothing that is a failure in the eyes of God. As you walk through your scariest places, know that you are not alone. You have God at your side and your team of teachers supporting you and urging you ever onward. If you fall down, get back up and try again, for in facing up to self-responsibility rather than blaming others you begin to see that life gets easier and easier. What is causing your fear must be learned in this life or it will be learned in the next one. You cannot remain off the Earth plane if you have not gone in and cleared your fears."

We must face what we fear. If we are afraid of something and hold it in our minds, we will attract it to us. In the laws of mind, like attracts like. If we continue to empower the fear of being robbed, we put out that vibration and someone can come in and do us the favor. If we're afraid that we can't trust people, they also won't disappoint us. It's we who are setting it up. If we're afraid of being rejected, we will attract situations to us again and again where we are rejected, until finally we learn that we are worthy of love and bring that energy into our lives instead.

Fear grows within us when we don't love ourselves. As we recognize the God within and love ourselves, we can learn to walk up to our fears with arms outstretched, welcoming the lesson they bring us. When we see these fear programs as teachers to help us grow, we can actually project a feeling of appreciation and thankfulness toward them. We look at them, learn from them, and then their negative power disappears. We can take control and transform the difficult situations instead of being ruled by our fears.

Our level of awareness determines how well we do in conquering any fear that arises. We should not expect to be perfect. We can keep working on the fear and applaud ourselves each time we take a step forward. It may mean saying no to someone, making a phone call to someone we'd rather avoid, facing uncomfortable feelings and verbalizing them, or just being honest and acknowledging that a fear is present. Overcoming the problem involves the willingness to face up to it. When we stop running from the fears we have empowered, they no longer maintain any power over us.

I took a class at a local college many years ago called "Twelve Steps for Everyone." This was a basic introductory course for understanding and participating in a twelve-step program. The class had about thirty students. When we came to the weekly session covering the fifth step—admitting to God, to ourselves, and to another human being the exact nature of our wrongs—the classroom was virtually empty. Most of the people were afraid to admit and share any of their mistakes, so they chose not to attend. This was a clear example how we can let fear rule our lives.

Major Life Fears

Let's get into some of our fears. The fear of rejection can be rooted in our past. We may have had role expectations of our parents. They didn't live up to what we wanted them to be, so we're still hurt. Then we go into our relationships and our partner doesn't live up to what we expect. The pattern continues, and this creates conflict in our lives. We already have rejected ourselves, so we keep bringing in others to do the same. If we release the hurt and forgive our parents, we can then change the program to a self-loving pattern.

Nothing can exist in our reality unless we feed it energy. By empowering our fears, we cause a tremendous drain of our energy. If we look in the mirror and say, "I'm getting old and wrinkled," we are literally creating that image of ourselves. If we look in the mirror and say, "Hello gorgeous lady, I love you," soon we will see ourselves as that loving, beautiful person.

The fear of abandonment tells us that we're scared that we are not worthy of love. We fear that people will leave us because of finding something terrible or wrong about our essential nature: We're afraid that if we show our weaknesses, they will leave. Realize that no one is perfect. If we play the "very together person" role, it will exhaust us.

Open up and share your mistakes with others. As we accept ourselves with all our strengths and weaknesses, we will give others permission to be honest and love us for who we truly are. If we can be direct and honest and say, "This is who I am and I'm lovable just the way I am," we'll feel better about ourselves, as well as everyone else. This way others can open up and show us who they really are as well.

Many of us have a fear of intimacy. We fear being vulnerable because we can get hurt and rejected. Yet relationships are our finest teachers. If we can change our perception by seeing each person we have a relationship with as God in a little Earth suit, here to teach us lessons, life can be much easier. We came here to learn—not to avoid being close with others.

Another block to love is the fear of failure. Understand that the purpose of life is to grow, to progress. There is really no way to fail in life.

We make mistakes, but this is how we learn. We shouldn't be afraid of falling flat on our faces: We will learn how *not* to do something. If we see what we created and how we set it up, we can learn to create better choices next time. To help accomplish any task set before us, we can proceed with determination and a positive attitude. Whatever the outcome, we will have gained strength and knowledge.

For example, let's say a person is afraid of failing in their business. We have to look at the fear, asking ourselves, "What's the worst thing that could possibly happen?" We could lose everything, go bankrupt, and have to start over. But the mind is unlimited, and what we created once we can create again with better knowledge and skill. History is full of stories about millionaires who made a fortune, lost every penny of it, then created an even more impressive cash flow. We grow from each life experience.

People can also have a fear of success. Underlying this fear is the feeling that they don't deserve to have success in their lives. They fear that they will be expected to be perfect all the time and others will expect only the best of them. Some religions may even have taught us that it is selfish to be rewarded with prosperity. Realize that we live in an abundant universe and it's our God-given right to succeed and enjoy happiness on the material level as well as the spiritual planes.

Another fear that people can empower is the fear of illness. If we keep ourselves balanced in body, mind, and spirit and if we clean out our fears and hurts, there won't be any need to set up a disease or illness. Continual stress tension and suppression break down our health. We need to learn how to recharge our energy and receive love, as well as give energy. People who give and give and neglect their own needs can set up long, debilitating illness in order to force themselves into learning how to receive back.

In our fear of death, we fear the unknown and that which we don't understand or haven't experienced. By expanding our self-awareness through meditation and the self-growth process, we will realize that there is no death. We see that our understanding of reality is eternally growing and changing. This opens us up to a deeper levels of perception in life.

The Last Fortress

My Guidance has called fear "the last fortress." It is the last stronghold we cling to that separates us from our true selves. We build walls around ourselves, fortifying ourselves, against what? We create within our own minds all our imagined threats and terrors. We must learn that there is nothing to fear but our own negativity. As we begin examining and overcoming our fears, one by one, we open doors to our fear fortress. We can tear down all the walls and blockages, allowing the love-force to flow into every corner of our beings.

This is true on a personal, a national, and an international scale: We must become aware of our divine unity and overcome the fear-consciousness that has separated us for so long from one another. We must learn to meet and greet every fear.

One of my fears I had to face was my fear of snakes. One weekend my husband and I went to a big party at a friend's house. I don't usually go to large parties, and when I got there I found out why I was there. We went out to the back yard and I immediately noticed a man with a six-foot boa constrictor wrapped around his body. I knew immediately I had been set up to face this fear and walk through it to pass the lesson. I went up to the snake and touched it gingerly with my index finger for a moment and said mentally to my Guidance, "Is that enough, can I go now?" A voice said to me, "You know that's not enough."

I went over and sat down on a swing near a glass patio table. I sat there wondering, "How in the world am I going to do this?" Then suddenly, out of nowhere, up pops the snake over the table, staring at me eyeball to eyeball, close to my face. Inside me, I heard the snake's voice say, "Are you going to work out your fear with me or you going to work it out with a snake who isn't so friendly?" Then the snake slithered off and I sat there for about an hour thinking about what to do.

Finally, my husband was getting tired of waiting and was ready to leave, so he went over and picked up the snake. I followed and went up to them and took the snake's body and wrapped it around my neck. Holding its head in his hands, my husband said, "Place your hands on top of mine and start sending it love."

I put my hands on top of his and began meditating and sending him love for all I was worth! He then let go of the snake and gave it totally to me. I heard the snake's voice say to me, "Do you not know that snakes are creatures of God also?" I thought, no, I hadn't remembered that. Then I knew I had passed my test, and was able to leave the party.

Releasing Anger and Resentments

From the mystic's viewpoint, there are no accidents or coincidences in life. Everything happens in our lives for a positive reason. We cannot bypass the emotional work that is necessary to tap into greater levels of spiritual awareness. Sometimes people take their knowledge of spiritual teachings and avoid dealing with their anger and resentments. They would rather just say, "Well it was just my karma and therefore I don't need to do anything about it." Denying pain and emotional hurts won't make them go away. Unless these are uncovered, acknowledged, and released, they will not be healed.

It's important to remember that anger is always a cover for our hurt feelings. Discovering our anger is a step in the process of healing. Once we hit the anger stage, we are very close to where we can examine the situation and ask ourselves: "Why would I choose that in my life? Why did I attract that?"

Verbalizing our true feelings is the key for opening up to releasing the pain. It's not healthy for us to keeping stuffing our emotions inside. We can at least verbalize, "that hurts," to others. By expressing our feelings, we keep the energy flowing, rather than constrict it. Otherwise, resentments build up inside and we can erupt like a volcano, usually at some small incident.

We feel much better about ourselves by verbalizing more. We feel a big difference in our energy fields, and that's exciting. Many of us who acted as people pleasers have always said yes to helping others when we really meant no, because we didn't want to disappoint the person. When we finally start being honest and say no, we feel much better about ourselves and have a lot more energy. When we express the truth and follow our true instincts, it is better for everyone concerned.

Transforming Shame and Guilt

The first key to transforming shame and guilt is to expose them. As the saying goes, "You're only as sick as your secrets." It is very important to express our fears and share them with others whom we trust and love. By exposing the fear, we remove the shame energy surrounding the issue. Keeping these problems suppressed inside only gives them more power. We cannot change fear into love unless we change feeling badly about it.

Exposing our weakness allows space for the light to embrace these dark, formerly forbidden areas within the self. Sharing this self-growth process is healthy for our healing. Verbalize about these areas with a close friend, a counselor, or a group devoted to this healing work. We can also picture a loving, wise teacher and ask for help and understanding in a visualization exercise, and release the energy in this way. In reaching out for help and support, we can learn to view our problems with fresh, new solutions.

Meditating daily will also give us the boost of energy to help move us through the blocks. But it is our responsibility to open up, expose, and release the areas that need to change. Ignoring the fears keeps the energy constricted and trapped inside. We may think we've worked it out, but whenever we get into close relationships, there's the old program rearing its negative head.

Shame is a feeling that there is something fundamentally wrong with us. We feel that we are flawed to the core of our beings. Our identities are rooted in a primal lack of self-worth. We are choosing fear instead of viewing our life situations as puzzles to be solved. We are identifying with the problem rather than seeing our infinite selves, which have an amazing unlimited ability to change and transform.

Ignoring the shameful areas keeps us trapped in our pasts and greatly affects our quality of life. There's an emptiness in our souls and we miss feeling whole and fully alive in our being. These blocks of shame can manifest as low energy, stress, immune disorders, depression, and overall poor health. Energy needs to be circulated through us in order to create. By removing the shame around an issue, the energy can open up.

To be a mystic means that we now invite the feelings of shame in order to see and comprehend their nature. Until now, this shame has held us back from knowing our feelings, intuitive abilities, and full creative expression. We may have hidden our shame by trying to appear perfect, thinking that if we're good no one can shame us. Others may have just withdrawn from people and activities by isolating themselves. We reject ourselves and we just wait for others to confirm what we already know—that we don't deserve love or respect.

Our positive affirmations will help us create new modes of being. In using guided visualization exercises, we can see ourselves handing back to our caretakers the shame we feel inside. By practicing greater self-love, we allow for healing these aspects of self. Through the loving support of family, friends, a counselor, or a group, we learn to share our difficulties and open up to receive greater nurturing and transformation.

One of our most draining emotions is guilt. It is rooted in fear, and like any negative emotion, it must be overcome. Guilt comes from feeling bad over something we've done. We feel poorly about some behavior or action that appeared to cause harm to others and ourselves. We must change our own way of thinking and our actions through learning from our mistakes.

Often our feelings of guilt stem from the fear of not living up to expectations or of looking bad in the eyes of others. Guilt can stem from fear of criticism from authoritarian figures, fear of being ourselves, and fear of change. Many of us internalized the negative reactions we received from parents, schools, work, and relationships, and continue to feel pain because of them.

Some religious doctrines also helped to program us to feel guilty. The idea was that if we do something wrong, we are sinning, and they taught us to dwell on feeling guilty about that. Oftentimes, our sexual expressions, desires for self-fulfillment, goals, and sex-role expectations were limited to what these religions dictated. We tried to live by these dictates, motivated out of fear.

When we commit acts that are harmful, we are ignorant of the ways of loving. Through the pain of these past mistakes, we finally learn better ways to love ourselves and one other. We need to identify the mistakes and feel their impact, or we won't know we're making poor choices.

Denying that these experiences happened just keeps us cloaked in the energy of guilt. We cannot erase the consequences of what we've done, but we can accept our responsibility for them. Then we must change our way of thinking and behaving that is inappropriate, and learn to make wiser choices.

Self-guilt gives other people the ability to manipulate us. We perform and behave out of our guilt program. Know that if we are behaving out of guilt, we are doing it for the wrong reasons. We're not helping or loving ourselves or the other person. We should act from knowing that it feels right in our heart. In this way we won't give away our power or control to someone else.

When someone asks us to do something that feels inappropriate, we can say, "No, that just doesn't feel right to me." If we make excuses, they will sense that we're not being honest. People can feel when we are not telling the truth, so always give them a simple, honest answer. We remain true to ourselves and that is one of our goals.

Guilt is also based on ignorance of the law of karma. It's important to know that we can't do anything to anyone unless they're setting up the situation also. We are each led into one another's lives to teach. Through trial and error we learn how to make wiser decisions and how to love more. We don't have to devalue ourselves or seek revenge on others because of these painful episodes. There's a jewel of discovery hidden in each lesson. Embracing the idea that we will gain positive insights about these experiences helps inspire us to probe under the surface for their greater meaning.

Moving Beyond Denial

Expressing our feelings and needs brings us out of denial. We need to move from repression of these formerly unacceptable aspects of self into conscious awareness of them. Healing these programs enable us to become more present and experience greater energy and zest in being alive.

We bury our emotions to deny ourselves, thinking that they are wrong or negative. No repressed emotion is lost. It just resurfaces later in various forms of self-defeating behavior. Avoidance of our emotions affects our physical health and well-being. It is the root cause of disease in our bodies, minds, and spirits.

If verbalizing our needs makes other people uncomfortable, that's okay. In expressing our needs, thoughts, and feelings, we will feel better. I like the saying, "What other people think about me is none of my business." By being honest and direct, we enable others to truly be themselves with us as well. We are giving them permission to say their truth in a supportive atmosphere.

If our previous role with people was to always place their needs and desires above our own and then we change the role, some people may not be willing to adjust to this new sharing relationship. These relationships were based on our caretaking role and are not "give and take" relationships. As I've said—like attracts like. We need to be with people who have a similar capacity to give love, support, and energy back to us. At the same time, we need to exercise patience and give others time to adjust to our new roles as self-loving beings.

To move beyond denial starts with the willingness to face all our feelings. Examine them without judging whether they are right or wrong, and decide what actions will empower us to attain our greatest good. As we separate ourselves from a lifestyle of blaming ourselves or others, we are then free to heal the areas we've hidden away in ourselves.

As we release and heal our uncomfortable feelings, a natural flow of energy begins to move within us. Because we denied our feelings, we became afraid of them. But as we accept, experience, and release the feelings, we forge new pathways for positive energy and light to fill our being. This is the way of the mystic.

Finding Forgiveness

Resentments hurt only the vehicle they're housed in. As we carry our grudges against others, this only sets up a constriction in our energy field. When we resist giving or receiving forgiveness, we separate ourselves from the God force. As we truly begin to see that others came in to teach us in this life, we can open up to letting go of our grievances. There is a reason that these interactions took place. We can forgive the others who hurt us in our past, and can also include ourselves on the list. Holding on to pain and suffering is a heavy weight to carry. We feel a tremendous sense of freedom and fulfillment as we lift this weight from our being.

What we sow, we reap. In reviewing past abuses, I always figure that somewhere down the road in my past lives I've hurt the person who perpetrated the act. In this life, especially in the first twenty-eight years, I'm paying back the karma. Rather than repeat this cycle over and over again, I'm going to release and forgive the person this time around. Then I'm free. It doesn't matter how they respond, I want to know that there is no resentment or anger inside of me.

Old souls are always extra-sensitive to the pain and harm people cause one another. This is because we've experienced these episodes ourselves in past lives. We've usually had more than nineteen incarnations here on Earth, so we've been through the gamut of experiences. Young souls don't realize the impact of their actions. They haven't yet experienced the pain and results of their harmful decisions. They see themselves as getting away with these behaviors and crimes. Mystics know that they will reap what they sow and that at the end of their lives comes a review of their entire incarnation.

Our daily meditation is there to raise our energy level and awareness so we learn new levels of love and understanding towards ourselves and all people. We're building an electrical circuit throughout the body that is healing and cleansing the system. The beauty about meditating is that all the guilt, fear, resentment, and anger towards self and others rises up to the surface to be released once and for all. We begin to see beyond the outer actions and find greater inner peace and contentment within.

Our Guidance will never bring up programs unless we are ready to deal with them. Once we see the negative patterns and change them, we will be tested three times to see if we have passed each lesson. Once we pass these tests, we are free of the pattern and can create a new scenario. We must realize that our lessons will follow us throughout this lifetime as well as the next if we avoid the self-growth process.

All people have hurt others, hated, and acted violently in one incarnation or another. No one is free from the pangs of growth through the Earth plane. Thus, as we learn to see ourselves as part of the whole human family, we feel the struggles, the joys, and the frustrations of all people. When we truly learn to accept the responsibility of our own thoughts, words, and deeds, we are filled with compassion and love for all people.

Practicing forgiveness is an ongoing process in our self-growth. We continually look for our part in each experience with others and take responsibility for how we set it up. We stop recycling our wounds and now create healing and unity in all our relations. We are not separate, and by forgiving people we reunite our energy and connect to the God force.

We free ourselves from our condemnations and find peace of mind and serenity. We are all expressions of the God force here to grow and establish better self-expression and loving communication with one another.

■ *Cleaning Out Negative Baggage* Worksheets

Man cannot discover new oceans until he has courage to lose sight of the shore.

—Shedd

I. Reflect on your daily meditation practice this week. What was your experience of meditation? How did it effect your energy this week?

_____

_____

_____

_____

II. Write down a dream from this week. What did you learn about yourself from this dream?

_____

_____

_____

_____

III. What affirmations and visualizations are you using? How did you do with hearing your negative thoughts, cancelling them, and putting in a positive affirmation instead?

_____

_____

_____

Releasing the Past Affirmation: "I love and release all past fears and resentments. I'm free to create love in all that I do."

IV. Lesson of the Week
Write down at least one positive thing you learned during the past week. Review where you reacted and look to discover a new way to respond as a self-empowered, loving being.

_____

_____

_____

_____

V. Letting Go of Old Programs

1. When you were growing up, what were your role models' responses to their own hurt, anger, and mistakes? What were the most positive qualities that they offered?

_____

_____

_____

_____

_____

_____

_____

2. Which of these patterns (positive and negative) do you still repeat?

Positive: _____

_____

_____

Negative: _____

_____

_____

3. What are some of the positive qualities and strengths that you possess that will help you understand and release these patterns? How have you grown from the experiences?

_____

_____

_____

_____

VI. Fears

1. Even though it may seem at times that we have an unending amount of fears and difficulties, there are actually only five or six major fears we have to work out in our lifetimes. Circle the three you most relate to and number them according to their importance:

FEAR of:	rejection	illness	power	poverty
	abandonment	intimacy	powerlessness	death
	commitment	addictions	failure	success

Our thoughts, words, and actions determine our reality. The Universe is a great mirror in which to see the self. Whatever you perceive and believe about yourself will be reflected back to you.

2. Which areas of life do these fears tend to surface in?

_____

_____

_____

_____

3. List an experience this week where you were able to identify a fear and move through the situation rather than lose your power.

_____

_____

_____

4. List a situation from this week where you reacted with a fear that is similar to one you experienced as a child. Review it now and identify what the negative program is behind the hurt, fear, or negative reaction:

_____

_____

_____

5. Whatever you imagine, you can create. When you make a mistake, visualize yourself responding in the way you would like to react. Remember to be patient with yourself! Write down a positive way you could have better handled the situations you listed in question 4 :

_____

_____

_____

_____

VII. Shame and Guilt

Here are some helpful tips in dealing with shame and guilt.

a. The first step is to be willing to accept responsibility for the pattern and to want to change it.

b. Second is to express and share what you're feeling.

c. Third is to forgive and release the experience.

d. Fourth is to make the commitment to think and create new behavior patterns that are loving and self-empowering.

e. Fifth is to have patience and take time to clear out these programs. Recognize that self-growth is a life-long process and doesn't have to be done all at once.

f. Sixth is to be gentle with yourself. We all learn much better in a supportive, loving, and nurturing environment. Criticizing yourself just slows down the process.

1. Now list a negative life experience from your childhood that made you feel shameful. Afterwards list a present situation that brings up similar shameful feelings:

_____

_____

_____

2. List a situation from your past that made you feel guilty. Is there a situation in your life today which reflects this same sense of guilt? Write it down.

_____

_____

_____

3. *Denial* is often a major factor in staying stuck in our old programs. Sometimes we'd rather stay stuck in our known ruts than risk opening to new ways of living. Denial manifests in:

a. Pretending the problem doesn't exist when it comes up.

b. Minimizing a problem's importance.

c. Blaming others for the problem.

d. Becoming irritable when reference is made to the problem.

e. Changing the subject to avoid threatening topics.

Name an instance this week where you saw denial in practice:

_____

_____

_____

Through the self-growth process you begin to see that your "problems" are all special opportunities for growth. By listening to your inner voice, you'll always find the solutions.

When problems arise, first ask yourself:

• *Is my energy low and am I seeing why?*

• *Am I comparing myself to others?*

• *Am I trying to manipulate the outcome of events?*

• *Am I avoiding taking care of my own health and well-being?*

• *Did I forget to slow down and not push to get things done?*

VIII. Exercises to Release the Past: FORGIVENESS

Working on reprogramming beliefs is not merely practicing positive thinking. Learning to be positive and open, working through all our negative baggage, means we first have to look at it honestly. Before we bring new furniture into the house, it is important to do a thorough housecleaning.

A. Make a list of the ten most important people in your life and write down the positive lesson they taught you. Even the person you thought was the most challenging always has a lesson to teach you about your self-growth and esteem. Our toughest teachers produce some of our most important lessons:

1. _____

   _____

   _____

2. _____

   _____

   _____

3. _____

   _____

   _____

4. _____

   _____

   _____

5. _____

_____

_____

6. _____

_____

_____

7. _____

_____

_____

8. _____

_____

_____

9. _____

_____

_____

10._____

_____

_____

B. *We shall do well to remember how much we ourselves need for-giveness, and to learn to forgive freely, judging no one.*

The most effective means of overcoming resentment is to generate forgiveness of ourselves and others. Forgiveness of others begins when we become aware of our own contributions to the difficulties in our relationships. Forgiveness can be done in the form of a visualization exercise. The person need not be present or alive for the release in this process.

Here are some healthy ways to resolve problems, especially when the person or situation is from our past:

• In a meditative position, feel or picture the person in front of you. Ask them, "What was the positive lesson you came to teach me from this experience?" Listen for the answer. Then tell them the positive lesson you came to teach them. Thank them for being your teacher. This exercise can also be done with yourself!

• Write to the person's Guardian Angel expressing all your feelings about the experience or problem. Then ask the angel to resolve the issue. Tear the letter up the next day and release all your concern about the situation.

1. Try one of the above exercises and write down your feel-ings and results:

_____

_____

_____

2. Whom do you find easier to forgive—yourself or others?

_____

_____

_____

3. How do you treat yourself when you make a mistake? How do you treat others?

_____

_____

_____

_____

_____

4. When you were growing up, what were your role models' attitudes to forgiving themselves or others? Which of these patterns do you still repeat?

_____

_____

_____

_____

C. Give yourself a pat on the back. Celebrate your achievements!!

1. What have you done well lately?

_____

_____

_____

_____

_____

2. Where have you made progress in your growth?

_____

_____

_____

3. What obstacles have you overcome?

_____

_____

_____

_____

_____

IX. Guided Visualization

I want to do an exercise now that's going to help us to release shames, guilts, and fears—negative patterns that we've picked up from our parents, our teachers, from everyone around us since the time we were very young. What we want to accomplish in life is to be able to forgive all people. We will incarnate with anyone we don't forgive, and set up similar situations with them again in another life.

We pick up a lot of other people's negative programs and their fears that they cast off on us. Just a simple thing like being told, "You're stupid," when we are children can greatly influence our self-esteem. We buy into that program and then we play that role throughout our lives.

This exercise is going to give you an opportunity to release the negative patterns and to give them back to the people they belong to. (Remember to record the visualization on a cassette tape in your own voice.)

Sit quietly in a meditative position. Take three slow, deep breaths, inhale through the nose, and exhale to the base of your spine, and feel your energy field expanding.

Now imagine that your energy field is filling up the entire room . . . Now feel it expanding, and you're above your house . . . Feel yourself rising even further until you're over your town . . . Look down on the town . . . Feel what the energy feels like . . . Now imagine yourself going out into space and looking back at the Earth . . . This is the same view as the astronauts would have . . . Picture the Earth plane below you and feel your energy . . . And now, while you're out there, let's send love to the world . . . Just imagine all the people of the world holding hands and dancing around the world together . . . Everyone is living in love and harmony.

Your positive thought forms can change the world . . . As you send love to the world, feel it coming forth from you . . . Feel the love going out and being circled back to you . . . You feel a complete sense of bliss and well-being . . . See ribbons of light going out of everyone's heads connecting all of us to the sun . . . We're all a part of the same energy . . . By sending love to others, you see how you are sending love to yourself as well.

Now, as you stand there, feel the entire universe all enfolded in your arms . . . It's very peaceful; it's very beautiful; and you feel such wonderful love and freedom . . . Now, imagine a brilliant light appearing in front of you . . . See it as a golden light, like a golden tunnel of light . . . Now walk into this light . . . As you walk in you see a very wise, beautiful teacher with his (or her) arms outstretched . . . This is your teacher . . . This is one who has walked with you throughout your life, been with you day and night, and loves you far more than you could ever love yourself . . . Embrace the teacher . . .

Now the teacher is taking you back to where you see your parents, . . . your siblings, . . . everyone with whom you have had an important interaction throughout this life—any friend, lover, spouse—you see them all lined up . . . And as you stand there with your teacher, he (or she) is going to hand you a suitcase for each of these people . . . In this suitcase are all of the shames, the guilts, the resentments, the insecurities, the expectations that belong to each of these people, not to you . . . For we're really just mirrors for one another to see ourselves in . . .

And I want you to start with your parents . . . Give each one a suitcase . . . Hand the first one to your father . . . Tell him, "Thank you, these are not my trips and I no longer need them. I'm giving them back to you." . . . And as you hand the suitcase back to your father, you feel a lightening taking place within your body . . . It's an uplifting feeling . . . You're getting rid of something that was never yours to begin with . . . As you hand it over, you feel this wonderful, uplifting feeling throughout your energy field . . .

Now hand another to your mother, smile, and say, "I love

you, and I'm giving you back your own numbers, your own programs." . . . And now imagine giving a suitcase to each of your siblings . . . (Leave a pause here on the tape long enough to do this, or add the words needed to act out the visualization with each one.) You feel lighter and lighter. . . .

Now go to any partner that you've had, or spouse, and give them back their suitcase . . . You're giving it back with love, no accusations, no resentments, just pure love—for it never belonged to you . . .

You're handing back all these old programs that belong to others . . . Now give a suitcase to any of your children, . . . any friends, . . . boss, . . . co-workers with whom you had problems . . . Hand them back . . .

You now feel very light, very warm, and very loving inside . . . And I want you to imagine yourself now releasing those people . . . You love them, you bless them and thank them for being your teachers . . . They taught you how and how not to do things . . . They have been very important in your life . . . Because of these people, you're who you are today . . . Your strengths, your energy, your choices, all come from contributions they made to you . . .

Now imagine you and your teachers are standing by the ocean . . . You're going to take all of your own negative think-ing, guilts, fears, and resentments that you've created this lifetime and imagine that you're tossing a suitcase full of them into the sea . . . All that remains with you are the positive lessons you've learned . . . As you release the programs, you feel a great sense of relief . . . Now you can just dare to be yourself . . . As you go through each day, to change what you don't like about yourself and keep what you do . . . The secret of life is love yourself, and then everyone else will love you, too . . .

Now imagine your teacher and yourself walking back through the tunnel of light. As you stand there, before you go, the teacher is handing you a gift . . . This is a reward for doing so well . . . See the gift . . . Feel what it is . . . Let it be the first thing that comes to your mind . . . Now embrace your teacher, thank him or her for the wonderful gift and for the time spent helping you in this life . . .

Now imagine yourself being back out in the universe, looking down on the Earth plane . . . See yourself floating down closer and closer to the Earth plane . . . Feel what your energy is doing . . . Now see yourself above your own home town, looking down on it . . . Now imagine yourself over your home . . . Feel the energy field . . . Come back into the room that you started from . . . Now close your hands into a fist, and open your eyes.

You can do this exercise again and again and keep handing back the suitcases. Be sure that all these old programs are released from within you.

Write down any insights you received from the exercise:

_____

_____

_____

_____

_____

_____

_____

_____

X. Assignment for WEEK 4:

- *Do* your daily twenty-minute meditation.

- *Write* down any dreams you have this week.

- *Practice* daily affirmations and visualizations.

- *Read* Week 4 and fill out the "Balancing Body, Mind, and Spirit" worksheets.

Week 4

LIFE CYCLES:
Taking Risks and
Welcoming Change

Life is either a daring adventure or nothing.
—Helen Keller

Cycles of Life

There are several major cycles in our lives which help govern our growth and understanding. Every seven years we go through major cycles of change, completing the old and moving into the new. Not only has every cell in our bodies been replaced, but we have replaced old attitudes and ideas with new ones. We are also subject to yearly growth and renewal periods. We move through points in our own lives that correspond to the seasons of nature: planting of seeds, growing, harvesting, and assimilating.

These life cycles and transitions are there to revitalize and regenerate, not to devitalize us. As we embrace the ever-changing ebb and flow of changes and movement, our lives become exciting adventures. We can shift our old ideas and patterns about aging to reflect a new, energizing future plan.

Seven-Year Cycles

Every seven-year cycle of our life is a death and rebirth process. With each one, we move into new directions and acquire a whole new set of lessons.

The first four seven-year cycles we choose before we incarnate. Before coming into this life, we sit with our teachers on the other side and carefully select the important lessons, situations, and relationships that will serve our growth best during the first twenty-eight years. From twenty-eight on, we are free agents—whatever we sow, we reap. We are no longer bound by the pre-determined choices. We can create anything we want in life.

The first seven years of our lives begin our transition from infancy into childhood and establish our basic orientation about the self. We are all highly intuitive at this time, with the right side of the brain more functional than the left. During this period, we develop our creativity, imagination, and psychic abilities. We use these intuitive abilities to determine how to get what we want, when we want it, from our role models. We use our intuition adeptly at this age.

From ages seven to fourteen, we begin to develop more of our logic, intellect, and left-brain skills. In school, this seven-year period tends to emphasize left-brain functions: reason and analytical thinking. Most often, we discontinue the process of nourishing and developing the intuitive abilities. Ideally, we would add the analytical functions, which are important to our adjustment to practical realities, and encourage the intuitive development at the same time.

All too often, from seven to fourteen, a child has changed his focus from an inner awareness to the outer reality. Oftentimes, we discouraged individual creativity and the development of the imagination, which is our link to the God force at this time. We often tell children, "It's *just* your imagination." We can encourage children's creativity and intuitive abilities by introducing them to meditation, which helps make the transition into puberty much smoother.

In puberty, ages fourteen to twenty-one, we are completing our physical growth, moving into adulthood, and bringing the individual into the realization of his or her particular physical vibration. The whole body chemistry is coming into alignment with that unique vibration. This powerful, intense rush of energy must be released, and it is important to help children channel this force into creative endeavors, sports, art, music, and physical activities. To help children handle and manage this force, we must also openly discuss the changes and sexual energy.

While girls continue to express their feelings and emotions, boys are often encouraged to suppress their feelings. I feel this is the reason that women outlive men. Sharing and communicating our emotions and experiences helps to balance and release the stress and strain of daily life. This creates a healthier way of life.

From the ages of twenty-one to twenty-eight, tremendous emotional growth takes place. We experiment with our freedom as adults to establish living situations, partnerships, and careers. This is the period when we begin to develop our first sense of independence. We grow at such a rapid pace during these years that our needs and wants are constantly changing. It's very important to keep verbalizing to others about the growth and changes taking place.

Often, age twenty-eight provides a major turning point in the awareness of the individual. After behaving as others expect us to or rebelling against it, we begin to catch glimpses of being free agents and ask, "What do *I* really want?" We have finished all the lessons that we chose before we incarnated. We have developed many inner strengths. This is the time when we truly become our own person, regardless of what we have been taught by our parents, teachers, or society.

Age thirty-five begins the cycle for developing our spiritual processes. We usually get a wake-up call from God. It's God's way of making sure that we don't stay stuck in old patterns. Many times we will have a spiritual awakening through a dramatic life-shattering experience with a relationship, job, health issue, or death of someone close to us. This is the time when we question life: What is this journey all about? We're not here just to blunder along through life at random. We have a purpose for being here. This is the time to find our purpose by going within.

At age forty-two, we get another spiritual boost of energy. The seven-year cycle between forty-two and forty-nine should be easier, unless we have really been avoiding our lessons. This is the time to focus on our success, enjoy our relationships, and expand our spiritual awareness.

The forty-ninth year brings up the same life-force energy surge as puberty does. There is a surge of electricity going through us. This happens for men as well as women. This is another chance to feel and really use the life-force to renew our bodies, minds, and spirits. It's a time of renewal, and our spiritual centers will begin providing the hormones and vigor we need to maintain strength, youth, and agility. It's time to get the higher creative centers in working order.

Women can experience hot flashes from this energy increase. We're learning to process more and more energy. We can learn to utilize menopause and make it a very positive experience. If we meditate through the menopause period, the energy should be much easier to handle.

From age forty-nine on we can reach our greatest creative rewards. The finest art, music, writing, and creative accomplishments can be manifested. From this age on, we can also reach the greatest spiritual awareness and acceleration of the growth process, especially if we are meditating. These seven year cycles continue to affect us throughout the rest of our lives.

Understanding Death Cycles

Within the seven-year cycles, the sixth year is a death year. This is a time of pruning, cleaning out, and releasing any attitudes, belief systems, and patterns that are not producing growth. It can be a challenging time of letting go of old programs. If you know anyone going through a death cycle, be calm, be patient and remember that he or she needs extra love and support. A death cycle occurs in these years: 13, 20, 27, 34, 41, 48, 55, 62, etc. The old ways of being must die off to make way for new lessons to come.

In looking back through our lives, we can see that people often marry, divorce, have children, make job changes and big moves in the seventh year of the cycle. We can look back at our last seven-year cycle. What changes occurred? People will sometimes change their lifestyles without really thinking about why they are doing it.

Two years before making the change, or in the fifth year of our cycles, we begin to examine what kind of changes are needed. If we start to do the clean-up work then, we will have an easier death cycle. If we haven't made the changes by the year after the seventh year, then situations often force us to face our old programs until the changes have been made. Ready or not, it's time to shift. It's also very exciting to know that all new lessons are coming in for us.

Embracing Change

Life is dynamic, flowing, and changing. All things and forms around us change. We should always be willing to move on, to love more deeply, and to learn new things. In handling the changes that come our way, we should not take them personally. If people or situations are led out of our lives, then know it was for our greater growth. Everything changes. This is the nature of the universe.

If we face the changes and welcome them into our lives, the transitions can happen much easier. These are our opportunities to discard obsolete patterns and usher in new ways of being and relating. The more positive our attitudes are about these challenges, the greater will be our ability to learn and grow with speed and enjoyment. It is our fear and resistance to the changes that create the pain and discomfort.

Taking risks involves moving beyond our personal limits. It involves opening up to new ideas and examining the ways we might be holding ourselves back from our greatest good. We begin to welcome the changes necessary to complete our transformation. Bless each opportunity to identify and release any self-negating programs or to make lifestyle changes that are necessary to help us reach our greatest spiritual growth.

Yearly Cycles

To every thing there is a season, and a time to every purpose under the heaven.

—Ecclesiastes 3:1

We also move through yearly cycles which help us to grow. Every spring when the growing season begins for nature, it begins for us, too. To help us grow, we are given certain lessons and tasks to master physically, mentally, emotionally, and spiritually. On a higher level of awareness, we have chosen these lessons. If we learn them, we move on to greater understanding and self-knowledge. If we don't, then they will be waiting for us again next year.

We all work under the energy of change, even if we don't think about it. Every year, whatever lessons that we didn't learn in the previous spring-to-fall cycle will be there waiting for us again in the spring. We can go though our entire lifetimes choosing to avoid our lessons, if we so choose. There will always be the next life, the life after that, and each life thereafter waiting for us, until we decide to get in there and learn our lessons. God is very patient.

From spring to fall the energy is high, and usually things happen so fast that we hardly have time to evaluate them. But with the beginning of the fall season and the coming of winter, we have time to reflect and assimilate. If we carefully consider what we have mastered and what we left undone, we'll have a pretty good idea of what will be waiting for us again in the spring.

Our lessons are as varied as individual needs and evolution. We may be learning such things as how to forgive ourselves and others, overcome our fears of rejection and loneliness, accept responsibility for our choices, develop a healthy self-image, use a dormant talent, become clear on commitments, communicate our needs and feelings, or love the weaker aspects of ourselves.

To help gain clarity on what specific lessons are being given to us, we can review any experience from the past year we thought was unpleasant or unhappy. When we are in a quiet, meditative state, we can bring to mind the experience and the people involved in the situation. Then we should silently ask: "What was the positive lesson I was supposed to have learned from this?" If we are truly open to seeing our part in its creation and no longer wish to blame others, the insight will come.

The growing season is a time we can run twenty years of lessons into one six-month cycle, if we're paying attention. Then, September 23rd until March 21st is our introspective time. (In the southern hemisphere of the planet, the seasons of growth and introspection are reversed.) The animals hibernate and trees are dormant. As the sap goes down the trees, it means the energy is dropping in us. We are under this same energy shift. It's time to go within. Our dreams also become stronger and more frequent as our teachers come forth to help us clarify what lessons we were learning during the growing season.

January is the lowest energy month of the entire year. People who are not meditating and have no energy can fall into depression during this time of year. If we are meditating, we will be recharging our energy every day, keeping it high. When we feel the energy dropping, it's also helpful to increase meditation time by five minutes daily. For receiving more energy during the day, we can turn our palms up and think energy circulating up through us. We can also go outside into nature, hug a tree, and think the energy coming back into us. Realize that there is an unlimited energy field to tap into twenty-four hours a day.

January is also the easiest month to die. Most people don't want to die before the December holidays and upset everybody. They wait until the energy is at its lowest ebb, making it easier for them to leave. Everything, including us, is cycling energy in constant movement and change. The secret is to keep our energy high. With our energy high, we can manifest anything.

Life and Death: Two Sides of the Same Coin

It was my near-death experience that completely ended all my old beliefs about the nature of reality, what life is really all about, and why we are here in the first place. For many of us, such an experience is very shocking, because we begin to realize that there is absolutely no escaping from ourselves! Life is eternal, and we go on and on, meeting ourselves, our fears, over and over, until we finally decide to love ourselves and work on our growth.

If we are ever to come to terms with the meaning of our lives here on Earth, we must learn to understand death. It is only then that we can see the total perspective, and fit all the pieces of the puzzle together. Of course, after we have meditated for a while, we begin to lose the fear of death, because we can tap into other planes of existence. We realize that we exist on many realms simultaneously, and only the physical body is shed at the time of death.

The Nature of Death

There is no *death*. If people correctly understood death, they would no longer have any fear of the unknown. Death is but an inevitable transition that each soul makes when it leaves the physical body. It is a freer state which does not limit the soul to time and place.

Death is a change in the rate of vibration. The energy force or soul which is the real us sheds the lower vibration of the physical body at death. The body returns to dust, because the etheric or energy body no longer resides within the physical vehicle. In the state of so-called death, the energy, our spirit, leaves the physical body and does not return. Our personalities, memories, consciousness—everything we consider ourselves to be—move into this other dimension.

What we think of as *life* and *death* are merely transitions, changes, in the rate of vibration in a continual process of growth and unfoldment. The life energy, God, underlies all experiences of life and death. We will never be free from the cycles of death and rebirth until we come to know this energy behind all appearances, all cycles, all stages of growth. When we know the source of our true being, we begin to identify with our eternal nature rather than with the stages we are going through at any particular moment in any particular lifetime. To know the God Self is to know all things.

Death may be thought of as a graduation. There are no accidental deaths. When one leaves the Earth plane it means the soul has done all it wanted to do or was supposed to do, and there is no longer any need to remain on the physical plane during that specific incarnation.

It is, in fact, more difficult for one to be born than to die. When the soul is born into the world, it must lower its rate of vibration to take on the physical form. It must give up certain levels of expanded awareness in order to learn and grow through the lessons of the Earth plane. At death, we may once again return to a higher and finer vibration.

Suicide, however, is God's Big No-No. Life in the physical body is the most precious gift we are given, for in it we learn and grow. We can realize that there is always help available if we reach out during life's challenging episodes. Our team of teachers is right there if we will learn to listen within. If we kill ourselves, we immediately separate from our Earth suit and are left in the same depressed emotional state without a body to work out our lessons.

According to my guidance, it takes at least 80 to 120 years to reincarnate, and we usually pick up two to eight extra incarnations for each suicide. Later on, we must go through the identical situation we were trying to avoid when we took our life. As for special situations such as "accidental" drug overdoses or suicides as an escape from severe medical situations, these are all reviewed on an individual basis.

Death as Regeneration

Death as a process of regeneration is an ancient theme. Traditions of old taught one how to die: the stages one goes through, and how to maintain awareness and experience the process fully. It is only because we have separated ourselves from the awareness of our true spiritual nature that the idea of death sounds grim and forbidding.

If we meditate daily, by the time we are ready to shed our physical bodies, the process of changing vibrations and entering expanded levels of consciousness will be old hat. It will be something we can look forward to after a job well done on the Earth. We can participate fully in the experience. It is too beautiful an experience to miss through fear or ignorance!

To see death in its beauty is also to realize the beauty of life on Earth. It is a great privilege to be allowed to incarnate, because here we have the opportunity to learn so much more quickly. As we continue this growth process, we eventually merge our consciousness with the formless, the God energy, which manifests through all life expressions, all forms.

Relationship Cycles

Our partnerships, businesses, and marriages also go through seven-year cycles of death and rebirth. In the fifth year of a relationship, we should determine what we like and don't like, what is going well, and what needs improvement. This is the time when the energy of this particular liaison is building momentum for change. And if the relationship is not growth-producing, it will most likely break up. Again, this is not intended as a punishment, or to scare us, but rather to enable us to do the pruning and refining that is necessary to maximize our growth and happiness.

If both parties are working as a unit, these cycle changes produce beautiful transitions into new and more exciting dimensions together. This is what each cycle change offers us. Remember that the purpose of each cycle and experience is to help us grow toward our highest potential.

Healing Energy and Cycles

Every seven years we also go through health cycles, just as we go through cycles in relationships, jobs, chronological age, and so on. Every seven years each cell in our bodies has been replaced, and our psychological attitudes change.

If we are aware of the various cycles we are in at any given time— job, age, relationships, health—then we can be more prepared when we approach the transition periods. The sixth and seventh years of any cycle can be times of additional stress if we do not understand what is happening. But if we are meditating, we can observe situations in a detached way, knowing that the old is passing and the new is moving into our experience.

My channel has said that it takes seven years for a disease to manifest in the physical body from the time it begins in our thought patterns. For example, if we discover that we have cancer or stomach ulcers, the problem may appear to come on suddenly, but in fact it has been building in our energy fields for a long time. (This does not hold true for minor imbalances or for colds and viruses, which are cleansing agents.)

This is important to realize. Disease manifests in the energy field before it manifests in the physical body. Some people can examine a person's energy field and determine whether or not a person is going to be sick, even when the person is showing no sign of approaching illness.

Of course, as we become more sensitive to energy through meditation, we will become aware of our extended energy body, and can detect and correct subtle changes as they arise.

We have heard that prevention is the best cure. We should become so sensitive to the balance of energy within us that we can eliminate all tension and all negativity-causing energy blocks before they ever have a chance to manifest as physical illness.

We Are Energy Beings

It is easy to understand healing if we think of ourselves as electrical systems. We are energy beings, systems of interpenetrating energy fields. What we perceive as the physical body is only one level of vibration within the total system.

Our teachers on the other side, and those persons who perceive clairvoyantly, don't see us as solid at all. They see us as levels of vibration within an energy field. They see how smoothly the energy is flowing, whether it is blocked, and how much we can hold and process within our systems. These factors determine our state of physical, mental, and spiritual health.

The body as vibration is fluid and pliable. It can easily be molded into a state of health or a state of disease, depending upon our thinking. Our thoughts move easily throughout the body, and every cell is alive with intelligence. We are constantly being built up or torn down by our behavior patterns and thinking habits. So we are always in the process of creating harmony or disharmony within. We must catch on to this idea that we are *dynamic life energy* if we would truly understand the healing process.

The energy that surrounds and interpenetrates the physical body is called the etheric body, or aura. But what is this energy? It is the life force, healing energy, *prana,* holy spirit, *kundalini,* or whatever we want to call it. The ancient Hawaiians called it *mana,* the Chinese knew it as *ch'i,* and it has been known in almost every ancient tradition. It permeates all life, it *is* life, and it fills the universe. It is the essence of our beings. It is God energy, or love energy. How we use and process it determines how we experience reality.

Meditation, Dreams, and Healing

Healing is a complex process. In general it involves bringing about vibrational harmony among all aspects of the self: spirit, mind, and body. Meditation is a connection process, and thus it is also a healing process.

The easiest way to keep our energy high and cleanse the chakras or energy-centers is through daily meditation. In the meditation process we are relaxing and bringing up the kundalini to heal and harmonize the energy systems of our bodies. People who seriously undertake meditation are likely to experience an increase in vitality and a general improvement in health.

What we call resistance to disease is also a result of high energy. If the body is imbalanced, in a run-down state, we will be more likely to pick up whatever is in the air. Negative attitudes, depression, boredom, and confusion dissipate the body's energy and leave us wide open.

Meditation is really the key to strengthening our own energy fields and our resistance to disease, because every time we meditate we are recharging our batteries. Each and every cell in the body contains inter-dimensional atoms of energy. By meditating, we're revitalizing every cell and raising our energy level in the physical and etheric bodies. We are keeping them light, and increasing our overall level of awareness. Negativity and blocks will be dislodged from our systems, because they are weights that cannot stay within an enlightened body. They will come up and out, and the hurts we have suppressed will have to be looked at and released.

People who meditate regularly may soon feel an energy flow from their fingertips, which is the healing power. They can become channels through which this healing energy can flow to their fellows. In meditation groups, this healing power may be greatly multiplied. It may be directed to a member of the group or to someone physically absent.

Do not hesitate to send healing thoughts to others. Vividly *picture* the person well and active. See the healing power of love surrounding him or her. We can do this any time during the day, or at the close of meditation when our energy is the highest.

Each of us is a channel for the healing energy, and the strongest level of this energy is love. We should always send love or healing energy to others, whether we think their illness is terminal or temporary. This energy can help to bring about healing, spiritual insight, or energy support for the person.

Dreams are a special level of inner visualization and insight and are valuable tools in problem-solving. Dreams give us a reading on where we are physically, mentally, and spiritually. They can show us which energy centers or chakras are out of balance.

For example, if we dream of being stabbed in the heart, we are losing energy from the heart chakra. We may be getting too involved in other people's issues and empathizing with them instead of seeing how they have set themselves up for a great learning experience. Or we may be giving love energy to a partner and not getting any back. It helps to pay attention in dreams to the area of the body that is highlighted, and understand the accompanying lesson.

Understanding the Chakras

To understand the chakras we first must recognize that there is one life energy, or God force. I use the term *kundalini* to describe this energy because it was how I have been taught by my Guidance. It comes from Hinduism.

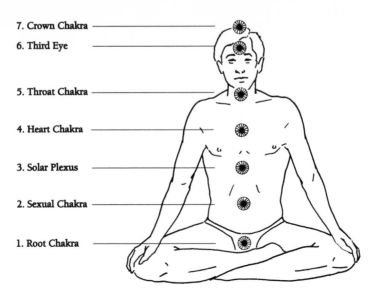

7. Crown Chakra

6. Third Eye

5. Throat Chakra

4. Heart Chakra

3. Solar Plexus

2. Sexual Chakra

1. Root Chakra

This kundalini or life force is housed in all of us at the base of the spine. This is our infinite reservoir of spiritual energy. When we begin to direct it to higher energy centers of our body, we begin to expand our consciousness and recognize that we are spiritual beings.

There are seven basic energy centers or chakras. The word *chakra* comes from the Sanskrit term meaning wheel. Each chakra is a spinning wheel of energy. Although the chakra system has been part of the Hindu tradition for centuries, only recently have we in the West become more fully acquainted with it.

Chakras correspond roughly to the etheric dimensions of our endocrine glands. The soul, or etheric body, is connected to the physical body through these centers.

The chakras provide us with the key to understanding ourselves as expanded beings. The centers are located in the base of the spine, the sexual organs, the solar plexus, the heart, the throat, between the eyebrows (third eye), and the crown of the head. There are many focal points of energy within the human system, but these are the major ones. How we see ourselves, whether we are in touch with the God within, depends on what chakra we are functioning from.

Each chakra represents a way of perceiving ourselves and the world, a way of perceiving reality. If we suppress or block energy at any of these levels, disease will manifest in the corresponding area of the body. Different diseases will manifest as a result of blockage in any given chakra, depending upon an individual's mental and physical make-up. Disease may also result if a chakra is too wide open, for we then would not have control over the amount of energy flowing through it.

Our health depends upon a dynamic balance of energy among all the chakras, plus a balance of the male and female polarities within. We must learn how to awaken and direct energy through our systems to maintain maximum health and well-being.

It is important to realize that all of the chakras are open to a degree, but we tend to operate out of some more than others. In each individual, one or two will be weaker than the rest, and it is in the weak or blocked ones that tension or disease will manifest. Emotional suppression, for example, will manifest as disease in the area where there is the least energy—a blocked chakra—and then can spread to other areas. Cancer, a result of suppression, manifests behind whatever chakra is blocked. This can be a result of tension, fear, negative thinking, or sitting on our own unhappiness and not making changes. It is the end result of our lack of awareness. The key is to open the system, cleanse and flush out the energy field with the natural healing processes, and release the negative thought-patterns that are responsible for the disharmony in the first place.

The Root Chakra: Puberty and Menopause

The life energy or kundalini is housed at the base of the spine. The first or root chakra serves as a trigger to release this energy.

In the first chakra there are no energy blocks. The first is like a storage bank for the kundalini. The kundalini comes up naturally twice in our lives, once at puberty and again at menopause. When the kundalini is activated at puberty, it is bringing the entity into the awareness that he or she is a particular physical vibration, and the male and female chemistry comes into alignment. In addition to being a time of heightened sexual awareness, it is also a time of creativity.

Again at menopause, which both men and women experience, the kundalini brings us another chance to use this life energy to renew our physical, mental, and spiritual being. A hormonal change is involved for both men and women. The energy often gets stuck in the second or sexual chakra. If this energy were truly understood, instead of running out to have affairs, we could transmute it into a higher level of vigor and well-being. Menopause certainly should not signify the beginning of old age, but rather that we now have a heightened creativity, which can propel us to the most creative and productive time of our lives.

These times of puberty and menopause can be stressful, due to the changes taking place; but through an understanding of energy and the practice of meditation, they can be periods of heightened growth which open the door to continued vitality.

Ideally, however, we learn to trigger this energy from the root chakra whenever it is needed, to use it to maintain a high level of awareness at all times. The important thing to remember here is that it is always with us as an infinite reservoir of vitality and strength.

The Second Chakra

The second or sexual chakra is the first one that can be blocked. Suppression of energy here may result from fears and guilts about sex, feeling inadequate in one's sexual role, having sex infrequently, being in a bad marriage, feeling unfulfilled in love and sleeping around, holding on to unpleasant memories from previous relationships, or trying to lead a celibate life and not understanding how to channel the energy into higher centers. The suppression gets expressed as violence, explosions of anger, prostate or female organ problems, colitis, and other physical ailments in the lower abdominal region.

It is important to utilize and release the energy in the second chakra in some way, whether through a creative outlet, sexual expression, meditation, or a combination of these. It is vital that we get in touch with our sexual needs and determine whether we are blocking energy in this center. If we feel a block in this chakra, visualize it and see it moving up through the body and out the top of the head.

When we first begin to meditate, we may feel the energy stimulating the life-force in this area. Many elderly people have resumed their sex lives after meditating, since meditation can reactivate sexual energy. Once again, the key is to balance and maintain a healthy flow of energy in this area.

The Third Chakra: Solar Plexus

The third chakra or solar plexus is the area in which most people, particularly sensitive ones, experience their difficulties. This is what I call the worry/fear chakra. It is a very vulnerable center.

If this chakra is not balanced or is too wide open, a person will pick up everyone else's issues, whether positive or negative. We may experience extreme nervousness, or find gall bladder problems, ulcers, or other stomach problems.

To balance this chakra we need to learn how to detach from other

people's issues, which is best done through building the energy in meditation, getting more physical exercise, and using the energy in some
creative outlet. If we feel ourselves reacting to others, we can always hop
up into the third-eye center, detach, and see the situation from a higher
perspective. What is the positive lesson this situation is teaching us?
When this center is balanced it can serve as a valuable intuitive guide,
for then it is no longer swayed by fear and anxiety.

The Fourth Chakra: the Heart Center

The fourth chakra or heart center is the first of the higher creative centers. This is the center of the Christ spirit, or unconditional love for
ourselves and our fellows. It is a beautiful level through which we experience unity with all life. But it has a dual problem.

First, if it is too wide open, we will pick up all the suffering and the
pain of the human condition. This can be a real problem if we are unable
to detach and gain a perspective on it.

This was one of my biggest problems: I would be so aware of a person's pain that I would try to solve the problem for them rather than see
how the person set up the problem and allow him or her to learn from
it. This leads to playing the mother-counselor or father-counselor role,
which is very safe. It is all right to play this some of the time, but we
also need to be vulnerable enough to see our own lessons in situations.

Second, if the heart center is closed or walled off, we will be unable
to love ourselves and others. Being closed in this center not only
blocks us from being sensitive to another's feelings, but may result in
high blood pressure and heart problems. (We build up and carry
around many resentments and hurts here, overloading this area with
unnecessary tension.)

The ideal is to be open and channeling energy from this center, but
remain detached and balanced at the same time.

The Fifth Chakra

The fifth center is associated with higher creativity and clairaudience
(psychic hearing or perception of finer vibrations), and is easy to block
through tension. Blocks here manifest most readily as tension in the back

of the neck, often resulting in backaches, headaches, and eyestrain. Rheumatism and arthritis are direct results of blockage across the neck and shoulders. Throat problems are also a result of suppression in the fifth center. If we have blocks in this area, we may feel our head tilt forward or back during meditation. This is helping to break up the stress tension in this area.

Other blocks are caused through lack of verbalization of one's real needs and feelings. Expressing our creative abilities and communicating with ourselves and others are important to the proper functioning of this center.

The Sixth Chakra: the Third Eye

The sixth chakra, also known as the third eye, is not a contributor to much illness. If a person has been concentrating for long hours, he or she may experience a build-up of tension between the eyes, resulting in a sinus headache or eyestrain, although these problems are usually a result of blockage in the fifth. The third eye merges into the crown or seventh chakra after a person has been meditating for a while, and the two are as one center.

The third eye is associated with the opening of true mystic potential and spiritual knowledge, seeing with the single eye of truth. When one has learned to direct energy through this center, the energy can be a powerful healing beam, stronger than a laser.

The Seventh Chakra: the Crown Center

The opening of this chakra represents union with the God Self. Pictures of saints and religious teachers often show a ring of light around the head—sometimes seen by poets, artists, and clairvoyants—which is the emanation of energy from the merger of the sixth and seventh chakras. This center is not associated with blockage and disease.

Mind over Matter

The real cause of disease begins and ends in our minds. More and more doctors are beginning to believe that a high percentage of illnesses do stem from stress: allergies, ulcers, cancer, diabetes, constipation, just to name a few. This stress is caused by a block in the system, or can be the result of a chakra being too wide open and depleting one's energy. Stress changes the whole chemical make-up of the physical body and alters the functioning of the endocrine glands and energy centers.

We are all a part of a great energy field, an infinite consciousness. The true self is a being of light and energy that is unlimited, healthy, and whole. However, we have wrapped up this self with beliefs, attitudes, and ideas that say we are limited and not deserving of our divine well-being.

Changing these attitudes and negative habits goes hand in hand with gaining control over our health and well-being. Any negative thought or habit blocks the flow of energy through our being and limits our perception and healing potential.

For sending healing to others or ourselves, my Guidance has always taught me to envision people in a white light energy, rather than to focus on specific colors. White contains all the colors of the rainbow, and if we send this pure light to others, then the body will channel it to whatever area needs healing.

One of my most dramatic healing experiences occurred many years ago when I had to have kidney surgery at the University of California Medical Center in San Francisco. Previous to this time, my medical problem had been diagnosed incorrectly. By the time I got to a kidney specialist, whom my inner voice insisted I try, I had already lost the use of my right kidney and was on the verge of losing the left one.

For two weeks daily before the eight-hour surgery, I mentally programmed, "There will be no pain; there will be no complications or energy loss; there will be minimal bleeding and fast healing." I also told the doctor that I didn't want any pain killers following the operation. He yelled at me, "Lady, this surgery is a 10! You're going to be screaming for pain killers!" I mentally said, "Cancel, cancel" to his statement and continued my positive affirmations.

Well, the surgery went great and afterwards I had absolutely no pain killers, not even an aspirin. I felt no pain. I did the etheric surgery healing technique described in this week's worksheets, starting as soon as I came out of the anesthesia.

I was the first person there to accomplish the feat of doing without painkillers, and the doctors and nurses were astounded. After the surgery, my colon didn't freeze, which made my healing go even faster. This event really demonstrated how we can create miracles with God in using our minds in a positive way. I was even invited back to the hospital to lecture many times about using these spiritual techniques.

Summary

As we go through our yearly cycles, seven-year cycles, and relationship cycles, we should remember that we create each situation in our lives to teach us something quite special. It's important that we continue to look for the positive learning experience in everything we do. Most of our negative experiences come from a lack of self-love. By learning to love and appreciate ourselves, we can avoid many of the conflicts we usually create. And remember that each cycle is designed to propel us toward greater understanding and renewed vitality. Thus, as we move through our total life cycle, we should become more empowered. We should continually gain greater self-insight and a greater capacity for love and pleasure.

■ *Balancing Body, Mind, and Spirit* Worksheets

I. Reflect on your daily meditation practice this week. What was your experience of meditation? How did it effect your energy this week?

_____

_____

_____

_____

_____

II. Write down a dream from this week. What did you learn about yourself from this dream?

_____

_____

_____

_____

_____

III. What affirmations and visualizations are you using? How did you do with hearing your negative thoughts, cancelling them, and putting in a positive affirmation instead?

_____

_____

_____

_____

_____

Affirmations for Health and Wholeness

As suggested before, affirmations are easy to use and can be repeated at the end of your meditation before closing down. Say each one three times assertively, getting into the feeling of well-being as much as possible. The following are suggestions for improving your health. Pick the ones that offer the most positive statements for you.

1. The natural state of my being is health, harmony, and wholeness.

2. I am in control of my life and health.

3. *I am filled with energy, vitality, and radiant health.*

4. *I am now recognizing and correcting all limiting beliefs that stand in the way of my health and happiness.*

5. *I love myself as a unique and creative person. I feel love toward others.*

6. *My imagination is the door to achieving my life goals. I imagine and visualize myself as happy, successful, healthy, and joyous.*

7. *I am free to create whatever I desire.*

8. *My mind is adjusting my body to achieve and maintain my ideal weight.*

9. *Universal love flows through my body, mind, and spirit.*

10. *I greet all persons with unconditional love.*

11. *Every day in every way my health, happiness, and prosperity increase.*

12. *Every night I enjoy a soothing, relaxing, and rejuvenating rest.*

13. *Every morning I awaken feeling happy and confident.*

14. *Divine love connects me to the healing power within me.*

15. *I am Loved. I am Love. I am free.*

IV. Lesson of the Week

Write down at least one positive thing you learned during the past week. Review where you reacted, and look to discover a new way to respond as a self-empowered, loving being:

_____

_____

_____

_____

V. Health Issues

1. List the area of the body (or chakras) where you have had the most physical difficulties this life.

_____

_____

_____

2. What have these illnesses or problems taught you about how to love yourself more?

_____

_____

_____

3. What changes have you made in your life to help release the blocks in these areas?

_____

_____

_____

VI. Balance and Harmony

Remember, you are not here to be perfect; you're here to balance yourself in body, mind, and spirit. As you read the list below, ask yourself. "Do I feel happy with myself and balanced in this area?" If not, focus on the area that needs help. Then relax into a meditative position with your palms turned up in your lap. Close your eyes and picture or feel a wise higher teacher sitting opposite you. Ask this teacher, "In what ways can I create more harmony in this area?" Listen quietly for the answer and write down what you receive:

1. Intimate relationships: _____

_____

_____

_____

2. Family relations: _____

_____

_____

_____

3. Friendships: _____

_____

_____

_____

4. Co-workers: _____

_____

_____

_____

5. Finances: _____

_____

_____

_____

6. Career:_____

_____

_____

_____

7. Creative skills:_____

_____

_____

_____

8. Health and body image:_____

_____

_____

_____

VII. Life is a series of changes and growth experiences. Your attitude
and state of mind concerning the situations you face determine

how easy and enjoyable your life will be. No one has any power over you unless you choose to give it to them. You can have inner peace regardless of your outward circumstances.

1. Name an experience this week where you were able to maintain your center and remain calm even though those around you were being negative or stressful:

_____

_____

_____

_____

_____

2. This week tune in and be aware of your feelings and impressions when you meet a new person or walk into a new environment. Pay special attention to how these impact upon your energy field. Push out a balloon of white light when you feel a negative impression. Describe an incident when you did this and its effect:

_____

_____

_____

_____

_____

3. Many of us feel fear when it comes to making changes in our lives. List three changes you've been through this year:

a. _____

_____

b. _____

_____

c. _____

_____

What were your responses to the changes? How did you handle these challenges?

a. _____

_____

b. _____

_____

c. _____

_____

What positive lessons or insights did you receive from making these changes in your life?

a. _____

_____

b. _____

_____

c. _____

_____

4. Look back over your life to the times you were going through seven year cycle changes; (7, 14, 21, 28, 35, 42, 49, etc.) Now list some of the changes and choices you made during these periods:

_____

_____

_____

_____

_____

_____

Congratulate yourself for all the growth and accomplishments you've achieved thus far!

VIII. Etheric Surgery

A healing technique that's wonderful to use is called etheric surgery. It raises the energy and heals the body.

Take your right hand and turn your palm up. Turn it at a right angle so that your thumb is facing away from your body. Keep your fingers together, your hand six inches away from your body and start at the root chakra. Lift your hand up through the body over the chakras and out the top of your head. Continue in a circular motion back down to the root chakra position and repeat this lifting-up process several times. You are clearing out any stress tension and healing yourself in all seven chakras.

This is a wonderful technique to use on burns and cuts, if you hurt yourself. Also, it may be used over wounds after surgery and for raising up people's energy fields when they have low energy. I also do this etheric surgery four or five times in a row before closing down at the end of my daily meditation for an extra boost of healing energy.

IX. Guided Visualization

One of the most exciting things in meditating is to realize that we can use meditation and visualizations to create healing in the body. Every cell in the body is composed of atoms held together by electromagnetic energy. As we meditate, we're not only increasing the flow of endorphins and hormones, but we're also bringing up an electrical force that is going to heal cells in the body. So by meditating daily, what we're really doing is awakening and changing the cells into healthy cells.

Here's a guided visualization to use for healing.

Take a few slow, deep breaths and relax . . . Close your eyes, and imagine a huge circle of light on the floor in front of you . . . See a spinning, beautiful white light . . . Now imagine yourself stepping into the center of the light . . . Feel this light merging into the body . . . It's going up through the soles of your feet . . . Feel it going up through your knees,

. . . your abdomen, . . . your chest, . . . and out the top of
your head, washing away all impurities, all stress and tension
. . . The light removes any disharmony or disease . . . Just feel
the energy permeating your body, vacuuming out all the old
programs that you no longer need . . . Feel your body lighten
as this energy goes up, through, and out the top of the head
. . . It looks much like a fountain going out all around you . . .

You're cleansing your physical body, but you're also
cleansing the energy field, too . . . Feel the light expanding at
least fifteen feet above you, underneath you, and all around
you . . . Just experience this energy . . . You now feel a complete sense of harmony and well-being . . . Now close your
hands into a fist, and open your eyes.

Write down any insights your received from the exercise:

_____

_____

_____

_____

_____

_____

_____

_____

X. Assignment for Week 5:

• *Do* your daily twenty-minute meditation.

• *Write* down any dreams you have this week.

• *Practice* daily affirmations and visualizations.

• *Read* Week 5 and fill out the "Checklist for Abundance" worksheets.

Week 5

CREATING AND RECEIVING PROSPERITY

Go confidently in the direction of your dreams! Live the life you've imagined.

—Henry David Thoreau

Our Divine Right to Abundance

Prosperity can mean different things to each of us. It may mean, for example, a new home, a higher income, a more fulfilling job, a meaningful love relationship, or an expanded awareness. To begin to understand the principle of prosperity, we must first recognize that it is our natural right to be rich, to lead an abundant life, to be successful, happy, and free. Our desire to be prosperous is a natural cosmic urge, a basic orientation to realize our unlimited, infinite self.

There may be times when it seems as if the good we most desire is denied us by someone or some outer circumstance. What limits us, however, is our lack of awareness that God's presence within and around us is meeting our every need. We are the architects and builders of our life stories through our attitudes, ideas, and beliefs. We are getting out of life exactly what we think we deserve—nothing more, nothing less.

When we begin to attune ourselves to eternal creative energy, abundance begins to express itself in all areas of our lives. We are inherently predisposed toward achievement, success, and self-realization. It is only our fears and insecurities—conditional, destructive thought habits—that cause frustration and limit our expanded awareness.

Success is a pattern of thinking and may become a conditioned process *within,* just like any other habit. By allowing positive thought patterns to flow through our minds, we create a sense of wealth, harmony, and completeness, and our outer realities will be transformed accordingly.

We are learning to express our God Self and bring out our spiritual awareness into the physical realm—not the other way around. Acquiring lots of material goods or relationships cannot make us more spiritual.

True prosperity is the development of a consciousness of abundance. We tend to limit ourselves by thinking that wealth and success are solely physical. By tuning into our inner resources, we can tap the endless divine wisdom, guidance, inspiration, and source of all our needs. The more we work with these divine ideas, the more we will expand in our spiritual understanding.

Imagination as the Bridge to God

The imagination is our bridge to God. It's our link to our true unlimited self. If we imagine ourselves as we desire to be, we will become it. This is our divine right. Our images of self determine our life's direction. If we don't like some aspect, we can change the image in our minds to reflect what we do like. See fat? Think thin. Feel poor? Think rich. Look old? Think young. And so on.

When thinking about how reality is created, we can realize that the very clothes we wear, our cars, our homes, our roads, our buildings, and our cities have had to be created through the right side of the brain first in order for left-brained people to build them.

So the imagination is the most powerful tool that we have. The saying, "As you think, so shall you be," is exactly correct. If we think that life is going to be a struggle, life will be a struggle. If we think, when we're undertaking a new project, "This will go easily and effortlessly," then it will go easily and effortlessly.

If we have a dream, we can create that dream. We create with our thoughts, words, and actions. If we want to be successful, but success is delayed, we must ask ourselves how we are blocking it. Maintaining high energy is very important for accomplishing our goals. If we're in a business, or starting a business, that isn't doing well, we should visualize clients pouring in the door. We need to keep our energy up by meditating daily, then see the goal, feel it in the mind's eye, and watch what happens. All we have to say as we do this is, "Prosperity is manifesting in my life now." We don't even have to believe it, and it doesn't matter if anyone else believes it either.

Prosperity Prerequisites

Here are some conditions to cultivate for increasing abundance:

1. A sincere desire for inner change. Change negative programs from within first.

2. Knowledge of universal law. An understanding that the nature of our beings is creative energy. We create our own realities.

3. Self-honesty. We must honestly face our inner poverty programs to begin to discover our true inner wealth.

4. Transformation of intellectual ideas into feeling. The intuitive self changes ideas into a living experience.

5. Love of ourselves for having created every aspect of our present reality. We must see what positive lesson is there for us before trying to move on from our present experience.

6. Remaining steadfast in our self-orientation. Persist in the daily reorientation of our minds and hearts to abundant living.

7. Acknowledgment that our inner capacities for transformation are endless. We must not limit ourselves to our present levels of awareness.

Removing Stumbling Blocks

We are unlimited beings who have been programmed to be limited. We can use our free will to create lives of growth and fulfillment once we understand how to direct our thought energy. We experience suffering in our lives because of our limited beliefs that we are victims of circumstances.

What we are really attempting to do is to break out of these limiting beliefs. Gradually, layer by layer, we must eliminate all the programs and thought processes that stand in the way of knowing our infinite potential.

Many people feel financially strapped, even destitute, and ask me how to change their lives by programming for prosperity. Their old program has been that they are stuck. They ask: "How can I get ahead in life? Improve my circumstances? Buy a new home? What business should I go into so that I will be financially secure?"

The answers, of course, do not rest upon finding the perfect profession, business, or location, or getting the lucky break. It does rest upon understanding the law of karma, the law of cause and effect. We more easily relate the idea of karma to our actions than to our attitudes. But whatever we think, returns to us. Whatever we believe about ourselves, consciously or subconsciously, becomes true. Our thoughts are powerful building blocks of energy. They do unto us as we do unto them. It is always those underlying attitudes that are our biggest stumbling blocks to wealth.

All those things out there that come along—the job, the promotion, the trip, the money, the new home—are images on the physical plane that correspond to the images we are creating on the mental plane.

When we ask how we can get ahead, how we can increase our level of prosperity, we must first understand that to increase prosperity means to increase awareness of our own inherent capacities and abilities. It is not a matter of becoming greater than we are now, but rather one of realizing   how great we already are. We have the ability within us right now to create and experience what we wish. The more we begin to practice and use these abilities, the more they work for us.

We must remind ourselves that poverty is not a virtue. We live in an abundant universe. Our creative energy is unlimited. We are here to grow, expand, and create on the mental, spiritual, and material levels. We have the right to express ourselves as fully as possible in all of these areas.

Negative thought habits and attitudes block the flow of energy that brings our rewards. This shows the importance of releasing ourselves mentally from fear, anxiety, and guilt in order to gain control of our physical and mental processes. We change our patterns by giving ourselves plenty of support and positive nurturing in our growth. Unfortunately, many of us learned to deny our right to success and learned to criticize ourselves endlessly as well. Doing these things creates a negative self-image and perpetuates our limitations.

We need to celebrate each achievement, give ourselves continual inner praise, and applaud each of our efforts to be willing to change and grow. If we can't take giant steps to changing old negative patterns, then we should take tiny ones and reward each movement. Any step forward is positive growth.

Focusing on the Positive

To use our vast potential, we need to access new avenues for developing our conscious awareness. Meditation can help us to awaken the unused portions of our brain cells so that we can tap into this unlimited energy source, deepen levels of perception, and understand a higher level of reality.

Our daily meditations, affirmations, and visualizations also help us learn to concentrate and focus on our goals in life. By learning to listen within and to remain calm and centered, we are able to hear and cancel out any self-defeating thoughts and programs. Also, meditation helps us to hear our inner voice's guidance and pay attention to the clues that are given to help us create our goals. Otherwise, our minds are busy and racing a mile a minute, and we are too scattered to hear any insights.

When our energy is down, we are unable to perceive life clearly. But as we build our energy fields and maintain them, we protect ourselves from experiencing negativity, confusion, and disease. We begin to see that life is a great, wonderful adventure, and we can enjoy the self-discovery ride.

We need to listen to our thought-forms every day and examine our beliefs concerning money and success. A common program people have is that one has to work for everything one gets in life. This is a limitation on how our rewards can come to us.

I like to use enjoyable visualizations to help create my abundance. Many of us were raised to think negatively about money. I've found it very effective to use humor to replace the old programs. My favorite visualization is to picture a huge herd of dairy cows in a barn, all hooked up to milking machines. Each one has thousand-dollar bills just pouring out of its udder, flowing into a huge storehouse for me. I use this funny imagery any time I need extra money, and it always works.

Another way many of us get stuck in our programming is that we visualize and affirm something, and then spend the rest of our time worrying that it's not going to come—or we get busy telling God how it should be accomplished. Our self-doubt and time restrictions on achieving our goals give the universe the message that we really aren't ready to let it just flow in. Worry constricts the energy flow.

If we stay locked in the intellect for a long time, we get out of balance and lose our energy. (Remember it is the creative energy that restores and rejuvenates us.) When we notice our energy is gone, we need to stop and do something creative, get outside, take a short trip, ask for support, and take care of our well-being.

In the Bible, Jesus said "In my Father's house are many mansions." All of those mansions lie within us. Each room has a different talent, gift, or ability, many of which we've never looked at. What we have to do is clear out the debris of the fears, the guilts, and the shame, and release them so we can see our own beauty. For we're all born as pure diamonds, but we wrap these tapes of negative thinking around us until we no longer see our own beauty.

In working with visualizations and changing our thought-forms, we begin to release ourselves so that we can be our God best, or our most creative self. This helps us to get through our lives. It also helps those around us, because they'll enjoy the light, charisma, and energy that we're putting out. And it's such a simple thing to do. As we play with the imagination, we begin to see we can tap into things far greater than were ever known to us before. And it's free. All it takes is sitting down, relaxing in a quiet time, and using and playing with the imagination.

Feel the Energy

I want to offer an exercise in which we can get a sense of what energy feels like, because our energy level is what dictates how easy or how hard our lives will be. With low energy, we get confused, we can't get answers readily, and we take everything as a personal attack. The lower the energy, the less the clarity.

> Close your eyes, relax, take a slow, deep breath, and feel your energy field. This is a light field that is around each of you. The further out the light goes, the more clarity you have and the more positive you will be.
>
> So, I want you to feel your energy . . . To begin, first think of a time you were really depressed, and feel what your energy field is doing . . .
>
> Now think of one of the happiest, most fun-filled times of your life . . . Now feel what your energy field is doing.

When we're depressed, we feel a heaviness. It's as though the energy caves in on us. We even walk with the body language of somebody weighted down with all the problems of the world. All we have to do to change the energy is to think immediately of that fun-filled time. It's as if the problem is lifted off our backs, off our shoulders, and we feel much lighter. This is transmutation of energy.

It is in loving oneself and radiating love that all good is drawn to us. God is love. It is a power. It's a force that is very, very real. As we meditate, we're going to feel more and more of this energy. The key is to keep our energy field projected a city block around, above, and underneath us. This positive energy field protects us.

Ninety-nine percent of people in the world are reacting to one another. They have no true control over their lives or their destinies. The first negative person they encounter in their day can drain their energy. By maintaining our energy, we can always stay in the eye of the hurricane while everybody else is going around and around. We stay in this nice, calm center where we can see how people are setting themselves up, and what their positive lessons are, but we don't have to go into the negativity and wallow in it with them.

Problem-Solving Exercises

Before going to bed, we can ask to have a dream that will give us insight and clarity into any situation. Then say, "I will remember the dream, I will wake up and write it down." Record the dream that comes between three and five in the morning, or the dream received just before awakening. The answer will be given. Do the exercise every night until the dream comes. Don't give up if it doesn't work in one night.

A good way to practice visualizing to create our success is to program our parking place. Before getting to a parking area, visualize an available space and simply affirm, "The perfect parking place is manifesting for me now." Watch and see how easily it works. This technique comes in handy, especially in crowded cities!

Most of us have been taught that life has to be difficult. Programming a parking space is a simple way to see how easy things can be if we let them. Once we let go of complaining and worrying about things, we can see how easily our goals can manifest. If we want a partnership, program, "The perfect partner is manifesting for me now." Do it daily at the end of meditation, say it three times assertively, affirm and feel it, and then release it and let it go. This can be done with anything we want: the perfect house, prosperity, career, abundance, health, insight, and so on. Anything we want can open up to us. Don't worry about how it gets there. Give God the creative freedom to bring it in any way He chooses. God can do things very nicely without us telling Him how to do it.

Clarifying and Empowering Goals

If we pursue our goals from an inner place of self-love and fullness, we naturally attract what we need and desire. It is our responsibility to use the divine energy and ask for what we need in our lives to help us on our self-growth journey.

Here are some suggestions for creating and manifesting your goals:

1. *Clarify the goal.* One of the most helpful exercises to gain clarity in your life is to write down the goals you either consciously or subconsciously held in mind when you created your present reality. That is to say, what beliefs or goals are now maintaining the patterns of your daily life? In recognizing how you created your present space, you gain perspective on how you want to set up a new one—how to formulate new goals. Deciding what you want is a giant step along the way in gaining a larger sense of your life's purpose.

2. *State the goal in the present.* Feel the goal as if it already exists. You can pretend someone is offering it to you right now; all you have to do is take one step forward. Do you have any hesitations or considerations? (What would so-and-so think? What would I do about this or that? I have to do such and such first . . . etc.) See what barriers or fears are standing in the way of "all systems go."

3. *State and feel positive affirmations about the goal.*

   Some sample ideas to use are:
   - This goal is for my highest good and the good of all concerned.
   - This or something better now manifests easily and effortlessly in the most perfect and satisfying way.
   - I thank God for this opportunity to actualize my goal and experience my creativity more fully.
   - I know that the universe is joyfully and abundantly manifesting my goal in my life now.

4. *Feel the reality of the goal often.* Enjoy the wonderful feeling of self-expansion that your goal has helped you realize, and feel your goal as having already manifested, as a certainty in your life, as often as you wish. It is especially helpful to empower your vision before going to sleep at night or when first awakening in the morning.

5. *Determine both short-term and long-range goals.* It is good to have both; they help to further clarify your direction, wants, and purpose.

6. *Don't take on so much that you feel overloaded or pressured.* Goals should inspire joyousness, eagerness, self-confidence, excitement, and purposefulness.

7. *If you don't achieve a goal, re-evaluate.* Did you really want it? Did it create tension and anxiety? Did your goal change? Do you wish to set the goal again, or release it as not truly being an instrument for self-awareness? Refuse to allow yourself to get caught in a self-judgment trap of "failure" because the process of goal actualization has changed from your original thought.

8. *Never take goals too seriously.* That means don't take yourself too seriously. You make the rules in your cosmic learning game and are free to go at your own pace, in your own way.

Manifesting "Miracles"

Ask, and it shall be given to you; seek and ye shall find; knock, and it shall be opened unto you.
—Matthew 7:7

Our current reality is the result of thoughts, words, and actions that we have empowered from our past. As we transform our negative attitudes and belief systems, our ability to attract our goals really speeds up. I've seen miracles manifest over and over again in a short amount of time. I know that God has always been there for me during the big crises in my life, but I have been truly amazed at the power of creation and visualization when applied to life's smaller challenges.

In 1984, I had purchased a new home and my front yard was covered in weeds. I went to my favorite hardware store to buy myself a new hoe for this project. As I was walking out of the store I heard a voice say to me, "You can go home, weed the yard yourself, get a sore back and muscles and blisters on your hands, or you can see it as done." I thought, that's crazy. It was a ridiculous idea, but then I asked myself, "What have I got to lose—except a sore back, muscles, and blisters?" I quickly visualized the yard as being cleared, and let it go.

It was a twenty-minute ride to my house and as I turned the corner and saw the house, I was astonished. The front yard was completely cleared, just as I had visualized it. I jumped out of the car and ran up to my husband, who was in the garage, and cried, "Did you see that? I just visualized that and it happened!" He looked at me rather dumfounded and told me that the owner of the housing project had come to clear out the yard of the house next door which hadn't sold yet and decided to do mine as well. I just sat there with tears of joy, filled with awe at God's amazing wizardry.

Another set of circumstances that surprised me happened in the early 1970s when I did a T.V. show for a PBS station. The show was called "Meditation: Turn on Without Drugs," and it emphasized the positive power of meditation and spiritual development. The show was well received and won awards for the station. Then, by some quirk of fate, the show was "accidentally" erased by a PBS technician. The station managers felt so bad that they offered me a three-part series!

I completed two of the three shows, and due to a power outage, our filming was shut down temporarily. Once again feeling sorry about the delay, the station offered me time to do a fourth T.V. show to make up for the inconvenience. I was able to get out my teachings way beyond my wildest dreams. This really showed me that if you have faith and work with God as a co-creative team, the sky is the limit on your success.

How to Circulate Prosperity

True prosperity revolves around developing a prosperity consciousness. With this consciousness, we come from an attitude of knowing that we will receive our divine good, and give thanks and express appreciation for its manifestation. We also encourage others to empower ideas of abundance and well-being. This increases our spiritual understanding for a more fulfilling life.

All people possess the ability to tap into their intuitive resources and creative talents from within to manifest their desires. Some people are more aware of their abilities to make wise choices and empower their positive goals. Many people get caught up in measuring themselves against others and competing with them for the same rewards. Rejoice in the well-being of others and celebrate their successes. This keeps your energy light and happy, to attract your good to you.

It's important that we don't limit ourselves by trying to achieve the same goals as others. We don't want to limit our rewards. I recommend that when we affirm our goals, we add, "This or something better, God," or "Block me if this is wrong." This is like free insurance that what we receive is truly for our highest good.

Be patient and keep affirming the positive. After affirming, release the desire and let God have it. Continue to create a loving environment for yourself and others. Push out love and surround yourself in white light each day. Cultivating a joyous attitude draws your success to you. The universe is there for everyone, ready to fulfill your requests so long as you don't get in the way.

Put the rewards to good use. It's important that we don't allow ourselves to be controlled by, attached to, or owned by the money or success we attract. These are only things—they don't define our identity. Money is simply green energy that buys us time to develop ourselves toward our highest purpose, and playtime to rest and relax. It's important to stay in touch with our divine source and be generous with our outpouring of good fortune. Share the ideas and tools for self-growth freely with others.

Most of us get caught up in playing the role of giver in our relationships, and never stop to ask for or to receive what we need. This is playing a martyr role. I myself had spent most of my life putting everyone's needs and desires before mine. As Jesus said, "Love thy neighbor as thyself." This means that we must be loving to ourselves as well. For true abundance to unfold in our lives we must keep the circle of energy flowing to us as we are giving.

Be gentle with learning to program, and take time to allow the process to unfold. My Guidance has said:

"Life is a river. You are all flowing down the middle of the river. Don't stop at the sides to question everything. You analyze, intellectualize, and worry your growth to death. Slow down your lives and learn to float easily in the middle, and all good will be brought to you.

"God has a way of leading exactly what you want into your life, if you will but ask. You feel that you are not worthy of asking for your prosperity. The God part within you deserves the very best of all things."

■ *Checklist for Abundance* Worksheets

For it is your Father's good pleasure to give you the kingdom.
—Luke 12:32

I. Reflect on your daily meditation practice this week. What was your experience of meditation? How did it effect your energy this week?

_____

_____

_____

_____

II. Write down a dream from this week. What did you learn about yourself from this dream?

_____

_____

_____

_____

_____

_____

_____

III. What affirmations and visualizations are you using? How did you do with hearing your negative thoughts, cancelling them, and putting in a positive affirmation instead?

Prosperity Affirmations

>*Success and abundance are mine.*
>
>*Prosperity is manifesting in my life now!*
>
>*My positive thinking attracts wealth to me.*
>
>*I delight in my success and I delight in the success of others.*
>
>*My success is assured.*
>
>*Everyday I awaken full of joy, energy, and creativity.*
>
>*What I imagine becomes a reality in my life.*
>
>*Abundance and prosperity are my natural state.*
>
>*Money is a healthy tool of self-expression.*

IV. Lesson of the Week

Write down at least one positive thing you learned during the past week. Review where you reacted, and look to discover a new way to respond as a self-empowered, loving being:

_____

_____

_____

V. Sometimes we get blocked in our prosperity because of a lack of clarity in defining our goals, a fear of change, and of taking new actions and risks, or a feeling of lack of self-worth: "It's really not that important. I can do without it."

Ask yourself: What do I really want in my life? List four of your most important goals for the year:

1. _____

2. _____

3. _____

4. _____

VI. We can also get stuck in empowering the habits of procrastination, confusion, or inaction. What are your present resources, creative abilities, and strengths that will help you achieve these goals?

_____

_____

_____

VII. Releasing Worry

One exercise I recommend is for you to carry a small memo pad with you for a week and jot down any worrisome thoughts you have throughout the day. Don't think about them, just write them down. Then set up a half hour each day in which you take out your "Worry List." Go down the list and give each problem listed two minutes of worry. When the time is up, you stop. You are not allowed to concern yourself with the problem except for this time. In this way, you'll find tons more energy and time in your day to empower your goals and let them flow in naturally.

1. Give an example of how you are programming a goal but may be blocking yourself with worry, self-doubt, and criticism:

_____

_____

_____

2. Imagine that you have just found Aladdin's magic lamp on your nightstand as you awaken from sleep. List three wishes you'd ask for, knowing you can have anything this life:

a. _____

b. _____

c. _____

Was this exercise difficult? Easy? Do you find it easier to ask for help and success for yourself or for others?

_____

_____

_____

3. What areas of your life are prosperous now? Where have you made progress in receiving your success and abundance?

_____

_____

_____

_____

4. What were some of your parents' ideas and belief systems about money? Which of the negative patterns do you still repeat?

_____

_____

_____

_____

5. Imagine what your lifestyle would be like if you allowed yourself to have everything you want. Describe in detail your ideal day:

_____

_____

_____

_____

Discovering and using your creative abilities can help you to develop confidence in your intuitive and spiritual powers. Some ideas for flexing this right-brain "muscle" are: Taking up a creative hobby, drawing, dancing, painting, singing, making crafts, writing, storytelling, writing poetry, making ceramics, traveling, flower arranging, studying a new language, learning a new sport, hiking, biking, exploring nature, playing with animals or children, or doing any activity that suggests pure play and enjoyment. These help keep your energy up as well. Taking a class or course in any of these things can help get you started.

VIII. Success Mandala and Prosperity Board

Do both of the following:

a. On the following "Success Mandala" sheet, list all the goals you'd like to accomplish (the perfect job, relationship, spiritual awareness, travel, house, etc.) Then color in the mandala. Glance at it often throughout the week. We've included an example and you can fill in the blank mandala.

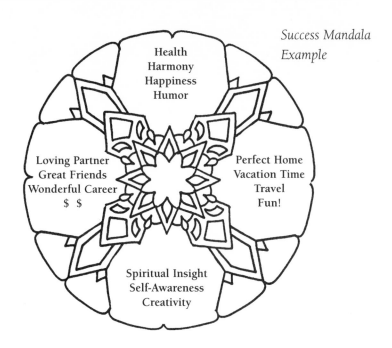

Success Mandala Example

Health
Harmony
Happiness
Humor

Loving Partner
Great Friends
Wonderful Career
$ $

Perfect Home
Vacation Time
Travel
Fun!

Spiritual Insight
Self-Awareness
Creativity

Success Mandala

b. Cut out pictures of all the prosperity goals you desire and pin them up on a bulletin board or poster board. You can go through magazines, newspapers, and travel brochures and use any images that create the vision of your perfect lifestyle. Hang this up in your house. As you pass the board each day, feel the joy and excitement of receiving all your divine good. Picture this board and affirm at the end of your meditation, "These goals are coming to me easily and effortlessly."

IX. Steps to Success Summary:

1. Decide what you love to do and do it. (Imagine yourself doing it, believe it, and you will!)

2. Create from within your own space—never compete with anyone else.

3. Rejoice in the success of every person. Never let envy or resentment creep into your consciousness.

4. Understand that it is right for you to want what you want and to have it manifest. Growing, increasing, and expanding one's reality is a natural cosmic urge.

5. Give to everyone more than you take. Give in value more than you charge in dollars. Then you will receive more than you ever imagined.

6. Empower the idea that your journey to success will be smooth and easy.

X. Guided Visualization

This exercise will help you to tap into some undiscovered talents and abilities that lie deep within you. There is an infinite storehouse of wealth waiting to be discovered. Relax and enjoy the exercise!

Imagine yourself in beautiful Venice, Italy . . . You're getting into a gondola, where there are four people to assist you and to make your journey pleasant . . . You're being treated as royalty, and it's very relaxing and peaceful . . . As the gondola sails off, you go through a mist . . . It's very foggy, and you can't see where you're going . . . Suddenly the mist clears and you find you are at the foot of a marble stairway . . . You're looking up at a beautiful marble building that you've never seen anywhere before . . . As you are helped out of the gondola and start to ascend the stairs, you see at the top of the stairs a very beautiful light-being . . . This is your master teacher . . . His (or her) arms are outstretched to welcome you . . .

As you ascend the stairs the teacher takes you off into the temple . . . As you walk into the foyer, you see that there are doors lining both sides of this magnificent hall . . . Behind each door on the left lies a talent, a gift, an ability that you were unaware that you had . . . The doors on the right are your past lives. Your teacher is leading you over to the doors on the left, and opens the first door . . .

As you enter the room, you're going to see yourself doing something that you've never done before, that you didn't realize you could ever do . . . What is this talent, what is this ability that has been unknown to you? . . .

Now imagine yourself going out of the first room . . . and into the second room on your left . . . And now you open the door and go inside . . . You discover an amazing talent here that is a gift for you to use. What is it? . . . What's happening in this room? . . .

Now imagine yourself leaving that room and going up to the third door on your left . . . As you enter this room, you realize there's a beautiful treasure chest in front of you that has all the gifts and abilities that were hidden inside you . . . Open the chest, and see what lies in there . . .

As you look at the top of the chest you'll see written on it the most powerful gift that you have within your grasp right now . . . What is written on the top of that chest? . . . If you can't get the words, see a symbol . . . And, as you realize, these gifts can be tapped at any time . . . All you have to do is relax, center your mind, and these will be given to you . . .

Now imagine yourself walking across the hall to the doors on the right side. As you come up to the doors, you realize that behind each door is a past life for you to explore . . .

You are going to go through three of the doors and discover what each particular lifetime was all about, and what your lessons were. As you open the first door and look into the room, what do you see? . . . Is it an indoor or outdoor scene? . . . Can you tell what country you were in? . . . What do you feel from that room? . . . Now imagine a scene in that room of who you were and what you were doing with your life during that lifetime . . . And ask your teacher, "What was my most important lesson in that lifetime?" . . . And imagine the teacher answering you . . .

Now, walk into the second room . . . This time it's a totally different scene . . . See if you can feel where you were. . . . What were you doing? . . . Were you a man or a woman? . . . What was the most important lesson from that lifetime? . . .

Now walk up to the third door . . . What was this lifetime all about? . . . Where was it? . . . What were you doing? . . . What was the most positive lesson of that lifetime? . . .

Now, as you come out into the hall, you glance back at the rooms on the right side, and you realize that any time that you want to look in at one of your past lives, all you ever have to do is open the doors. For all of your past lives are available for you, . . . and the bridge to seeing them is the imagination. You take the lessons that you learned from those lifetimes and you incorporate them into what you are doing in and with your life now . . . You can have any dream that you imagine . . . The pathway lies within.

Your teacher leads you back out of the temple, . . . onto the stairs . . . You descend the stairs, and step back into the gondola . . . And this time, as you go back through the fog, you know you will remember what you have learned, and you will be able to go back there at will . . . Now close your hands into a fist, and open your eyes.

Write down any insights you received from the exercise:

_____

_____

_____

_____

_____

_____

_____

XI. Assignment for Week 6:

- *Do* your daily twenty-minute meditation.

- *Write* down any dreams you have this week.

- *Practice* daily affirmations and visualizations.

- *Read* Week 6 and fill out the "Qualities of Love" worksheets.

Week 6

RELATIONSHIPS:
Mirrors to Self-Discovery

No one can make you feel inferior without your permission.
—Eleanor Roosevelt

Our Greatest Teachers

Interpersonal relationships provide our greatest opportunities for growth on the Earth plane. Each relationship shows us something about ourselves. We draw people to us in life to whom we will react, revealing old, inner programming about ourselves and the world we live in. The reason we have incarnated is to find out what's going on inside us and to clear out useless or negative beliefs. Our programs, energy level, and dominant chakra are the major contributing factors to how we interpret what's going on in our lives.

The first key to success in any of our relationships is communication. We must establish ways of relating where both people can express themselves, explore, and be supported in their growth processes. To do this, we have to be willing to listen intently to one another and make sure the right message is being heard and received.

Genuine communication begins with genuine respect for the other person as an infinite being and one who is willing to participate with us in life's learning process. The next element is commitment. We need to understand the level of commitment of both parties, the ground rules for operation, and what our limits are. Each person should be concerned for the benefit and well-being of both him or herself and the partner, as well as committed to working through problems and keeping lines of communication open. Of course, these can change and expand as we go along, but there needs to be a sense of commitment and agreement for harmony to prevail.

Two other ingredients for success in relationships are appreciation and acceptance. We won't survive very long in a situation if we feel unappreciated. We need to let our partners know how much we value their good qualities and recognize their specialness as individuals. We don't have to like all their qualities or agree with their choices, but we do need to share how much we love and care about them as fellow expressions of the God energy. Unconditional love allows us to function more freely as people and enables others to do so, too.

When we can accept ourselves with our weak areas, then we are free to be exactly who we are in our relationships, and we stop trying to earn others' love. Love is already the condition. We just have to rest in it. If people don't like us for who we are, that's okay. Others will be led in who do appreciate us. What we usually discover is that when we dare to love ourselves and be honest, people are drawn to us like to a magnet. This is the peace of mind we are all searching for—it's true love.

People love to be needed. Most of us are good at giving energy, but poor at receiving it. In accepting from others, we not only learn how to receive, we also allow those who give to us to feel good as well. If we need a hug, or need someone to be our sounding board, we give another person the opportunity to give to us. If we are given a compliment, learn to smile and say, "Thank you."

Blocks in Relationships

We will not be able to develop our mystical gifts if we are busy trying to fix another person's problems so we can feel happy and fulfilled. Many people are distracting themselves from their own difficulties and growth at hand by trying to change other people's behavior. We don't want to feel another's pain, so we try to correct it. We need to realize that until people are willing to go within and change their own hurts, fears, and negative programs, they aren't ready to grow.

A mystic encourages people to believe in themselves and to go within to find their own answers. People spend their time trying to correct others because they're avoiding the unhappiness within themselves. To really love someone is to accept them unconditionally as they are today.

One night, I asked my Guidance about a problem that my husband was avoiding. I was becoming annoyed. A teacher actually appeared to me in the room and said,

"You teach others not to judge other people, yet you, with the one you love the most, are judging him. Look rather at your own weaknesses and frailties, for you will be judged on these as he will be on his. Your spouse works hard to set up the mess he's in. It's his opportunity for self-growth. You never give him the privilege of learning his lesson, because you're selfish, Betty. You go in to fix it, so you don't have to feel his pain. It's his test—not yours!"

He went on and on, but I had already gotten the point! At the very end he said, *"And I am not your teacher. I am his."* This really showed me how we are truly responsible only for our own growth.

Clearing Past Relationships

As we do clean out these patterns from our past we're uplifted. This cleansing creates greater freedom of choices in our current relationships because we now have a fresh perspective. We can see clearly, because our eyes aren't colored by an unhealthful past distorting the present circumstances out of proportion. If our spouse behaves in some manner that makes us feel uncomfortable and hurt, we can work on that current, specific problem without being impeded by our past scenarios. We can save tons of time by being focused in the present. Life becomes much clearer and simpler to understand.

How do we know when we're clear with someone from our past? — When we can see the person without it bothering us. We can also clear our relationships through visualization exercises. These are especially useful for letting go of relationships where people have gone away or have died. I ask for the positive lesson they taught me, and also I like to say to them, "I love and release you to your highest good; you love and release me to mine." This is a powerful way to clear the lesson and let go of resentful energy.

When we can see people with whom we've had difficult relationships and not react, we can love them for who they are. Our goal is self-responsibility and self-discipline. See how we are creating our lives! It's us doing it to ourselves. It's not somebody out there. To get rid of the martyr and victim roles, we focus on knowing and changing ourselves.

Love, joy, and abundance await us, but they may not come through the specific persons or situations we had in mind. We must be willing to release ourselves and others into God's care, trusting that we will find what we seek, and that all things are working together for our good.

Importance of Friendship

Relationships in the new age require the solid foundation of friendship. All true heart-to-heart marriage relationships have always been based on friendship. Once again, we are all beginning to recognize an ancient truth. Sexual attraction without friendship is like a tree without roots. Initially, there's a lot of energy and the tree shoots up, but the first storm that comes along knocks it over.

Jumping into a sexual relationship with someone before we develop a friendship puts an extra burden on both people. We become immediately vulnerable and fearful, because we haven't developed the sense of trust and confidence in one another. We then can become fearful of losing the other's approval, and so we are on our best behavior. Immediate sexual involvement makes it difficult to maintain a sense of detachment and objectivity, and all too often destroys a potential friendship.

If we take our time and build strong levels of communication, we will learn a great deal about the other person without the rose-colored glasses. We can find out about ideas, goals, background, personality traits, spiritual orientation, self-awareness, problems, and so on, and determine whether we would be compatible as partners. At the very least, we have made a good friend. My Guidance recommends that we ideally spend 3–4 months together, as friends first, before becoming sexually intimate.

When we fall in love with someone, we need to take a look at the role we are playing with them. Every person with whom we're in a relationship—friends, lovers, spouses, parents, co-workers—has been in a past life with us. We can stop and say, "What are the roles that we are playing together now?"

If we've been the parent in the past, and now we're trying to work out an equal relationship, there can be adjustments in shifting to the co-creative partner role. No one enjoys being with a corrective know-it-all. When we change the roles, we can then go in and release the old way of being. The whole point in being life partners is to be best friends. We want to provide balanced support for one another on deep emotional and spiritual levels, honoring, appreciating, and encouraging one another. By putting the emphasis on friendship, we are opening to depths in one another that are rarely shared and nurtured.

Dance of Intimacy

The first step in learning the dance of intimacy with others is getting the steps down with oneself. We have to love and value ourselves before we can express intimacy with someone else. Sharing intimacy with another is having the ability to let someone into all aspects of the self—not just the comfortable, together-looking parts. We also share the weak, ignorant, and fearful parts of self. In loving another, we expose all the ideas, attitudes, and beliefs about ourselves. In this way we learn to love one another and help to transform the areas that need work.

True intimacy is a two-way street. Both partners are willing to support one another in the growth process. We can only change ourselves, and are not in relationships to force others to grow with us. If we draw to ourselves partners who are unwilling to take responsibility and who are being self-destructive, we need to question our own self-esteem, in that we choose someone who can't give back to us.

If you want to know how you are as an intimate partner, listen to and watch yourself for a week. How do you treat yourself? How do you respond to your own mistakes? Do you measure yourself against others? What do you see when you look in the mirror? You can only love and accept others to the degree you love and accept yourself. If you wish that others were more patient and tolerant of you, practice being this way with yourself. If you want to receive more love from the outside, practice loving yourself on the inside.

Defining Healthy Relationships

Our partner is our best mirror for getting to know ourselves. Ideally, our partner is our best friend, lover, and playmate, rolled into one. Initially, during the first phase of our relationships, we fall in love with the beauty and potential we see in one another. We project only the most positive and highest images on one another. We feel like we're soaring and are filled with a new sense of well-being.

As time goes by, our insecurities and weaknesses begin to surface. At this point, most of us tend to blame our partner and begin to find faults with him or her. All too often the relationship ends because we're afraid to go within to expose and work on the areas that need attention. But in a real relationship, this is where the work begins. We practice daily communication of our needs and processes and embrace the gift of having these negative programs reflected to us so we can transform them. This is a tremendous opportunity to truly learn to love ourselves and others.

A partner does not have to have the same spiritual beliefs as we do. As long as both parties are committed to living love and being responsible for their own issues, the relationship can flourish. Both people have to be coming from their hearts, not just their heads. If a person refuses to open up, and remains walled off from sharing feelings, there can be no true union of the love energy.

As our love and commitment grow, we begin to experience a true heart-to-heart union. My channel has expressed that there are very few true marriages or love energy unions on the Earth plane. The true marriage, whether legalized or not, is a physical, mental, and spiritual bond.

Both persons can advance toward self-understanding and enlightenment at a rapid pace. Love is shared and experienced by a blending of energies from all the chakras, enabling both partners to soar to new heights.

The expansive energy field that results from a loving commitment between partners can accelerate spiritual understanding. Feeding one another with this love energy enhances our awareness and ability to prosper and attract our greatest goals. We are there to work together to manifest the God consciousness individually and collectively, manifest the greatest talents and abilities, and achieve the greatest growth possible together in this lifetime. The sky is truly the limit when two beings unite in a heart-to-heart relationship.

Sexuality and the Mystic

We can each remain safe and in control of our reactions when we are alone. It's those challenging partnerships that get us to react—so we can see how spiritual we are when our buttons are jammed! This is why my Guidance has said that a heart-to-heart relationship based on equality is an important vehicle for growth and spiritual development. In order to show that we can maintain our balance in body, mind, and spirit, we each need to be in a partnership for a seven-year period. It's easy be to alone and celibate and talk about how spiritual we are.

The sexual energy is our life force, and we have to learn to direct it, both for fulfillment in our relationships and for awakening our higher intuitive abilities. Our sexuality is the closest way we can express love to our partner and experience God consciousness. When two beings join in the love-bond properly, out of a deep sense of love and commitment, they will experience an out-of-the-body merger with the God force. They are recharged and revitalized.

Particularly in the culture we are living in, which largely focuses on the exploitation of sex, it's imperative that we see the true purpose of sex, and transmute this energy for evolving into higher consciousness. It's the misuse of this second-chakra energy that is causing much of the destruction and violence in the world today.

In a true heart-to-heart union there must be a commitment to be sexually faithful to one another. If a partner is unfaithful, this breaks the energy bond, and sooner or later it is going to cause hurt and heartache to one or both partners. The foundation of our relationships must be based on trust and honesty. There is also the potential risk of acquiring and spreading a sexual disease in this day and age. Infidelity brings an imbalance to the union.

Developing Communication Skills

Whether with a spouse, distant relative, co-worker, child, or friend, we must establish ways of communicating so that everyone can express the full range of feelings and needs. We must be able to talk about and improve our interactions with others, and communicate the new ideas, feelings, and needs we discover. No matter what kind of a relationship we're presently involved in, the pathway to success is communication.

Realize that no one can hurt us, use us, reject us, or dump on us, unless we have set them up to do it. Understanding this really removes the resentments that we harbor and carry around. When we are truly loving ourselves, others are drawn to love us, too. Try it. Watch when people are dumping on you and ask, "How am I setting it up?" They are picking up on your vibrations that tell them you are expecting it.

If we learn to clean up the old negative patterns, then we can verbalize to others: "Hey, this is who I am. Love me or don't love me, but I love myself." No one wants us to be perfect. Some people try to act as if they are perfect or always right. They come across as very powerful and they let you know how "together" they are. People are unlikely to seek them out as true friends. If we share our mistakes in life, others will come and share theirs as well. That is how we learn from one another. Remember, in any situation, go with what the inner voice says. Take what feels right intuitively, and release the rest.

True success in communication depends on true seeing. We need to teach people who we are and what our needs and expectations are. We can ask if they hear and understand us, and if they are willing to meet our needs. Then see if they follow through with their actions. If they choose not to try to work with us and meet our needs (as we are working to meet theirs) then we can make the choice to go on and lead in others who are willing to work on the growth with us. If a partner is willing to go to counseling to help develop these skills, this can be a way to restore the love energy into the relationship.

The mystic sees our experiences as our way of learning. If we or others have made poor choices in partners, we can forgive ourselves and them and move on. We attract others to teach us, and vice versa. To see the error of our ways and not change, is not self-loving. To be a responsible person is to change what we don't like.

Laughter as a Tool

One of the greatest things to remember when dealing with the emotions is a sense of humor. A sense of humor is important in overcoming our fears and negative feelings. Being able to laugh at our own mistakes has an uplifting, balancing effect. When we are depressed, we often fail to see the lesson we were meant to learn. But if we can laugh and look at the situation light-heartedly, the lesson will shine through and we will grow beyond it. We can learn to say anything with love and humor. As Jean Cocteau said, "Angels can fly because they take themselves lightly."

If someone is being a bear at work or at home, we can smile and say something uplifting such as, "Having a bad day, are you? Is there anything I can do to help?" When we have to verbalize about a difficult situation, it's always helpful to try using humor and positive energy in expressing our ideas. Imagine how a favorite comedian might express the problem. Take an overview of the situation and see how important the problem really is in the scheme of things. Getting things in perspective makes it easier for everyone to find the solutions.

Understanding Emotions

Most negative emotions arise from self-doubt and insecurity. Feeling a lack results in some of the following behaviors: acting like a submissive victim, being a perfectionist, exaggerating and bragging, being highly critical of others, rigidly controlling self or others, and trying to keep everyone happy to buy ourselves peace and harmony.

Without daily meditation and the self-growth process, we go up and down with each mood swing, whether it is ours or another's. The trick is to recognize emotions and use them as tools for self-growth. No one can cause emotions in another. If we want to truly understand ourselves, we must be open and accepting of our emotional responses. This openness lets us see where we need work when we do react. There is nothing to fear about emotions themselves.

People who suppress their emotions will often just come from their intellects. They can tell you what they think about everything, but they don't allow for the expression of their own feelings and vulnerable areas. They seem to have it all together, but in fact it's as if they are going through life wearing coats of armor. When communicating with such people, we can express that we know what they think, but would they please tell us what they *feel* in regards to the issue.

We all have the ability to experience the full gamut of emotions, so it's important we don't righteously judge another person's reactions. We're each learning in different ways and different time frames. We can't change anyone but ourselves, so we need to keep focusing on our lessons. We have a full-time job with our own self-growth!

Whenever you feel uptight, try this calming technique to get you through a difficult situation:

Close your eyes and visualize an inner pool or lake, and observe what it looks like. If the water is choppy or wavy, imagine that you are spreading your hand across the lake and stilling the waters, calming the turmoil. Your emotional state will calm down in the process. Or if the lake you visualize is clear and peaceful, simply dwell on that image and allow the serenity to spread throughout your body and mind.

If you suddenly feel beset by problems coming at you from all directions, you can do this guided imagery exercise:

Imagine yourself as a giant rock, with sea waves crashing all around you. The waves may break over you, but you are firm and strong and can ride out any storm. Then, imagine that the sea around you is quieting down, and you see clearly in all directions. Your perception is enhanced, and you know exactly what steps to take to handle any and all situations.

Handling Negativity

I was always a very sensitive and psychic person. Before I meditated, I couldn't be in a crowd of people without feeling sick. I was tuned in to everyone's energy field. Oftentimes, there weren't a lot of positive people out there. Daily meditation taught me how to turn my intuitive switch on and off. I gained control over whether I chose to feel people's energy states or not. In this way, I didn't get pulled into someone else's negative influence.

Sometimes parents or people in our lives choose to dump on us because they love and trust us the most. When they're hurting and need to release the pain, they may pick on the person who seems most able to take it. To transform their energy, we can visualize them in a white light, and also place a white light around ourselves. In addition, we can picture them at the end of our meditation and mentally say, "Divine love and divine order are manifesting in this situation now." Say it assertively three times, and do it every single day. The situation will be transformed. We're giving it to God and God will take care of it.

If we happen to be around someone who is angry or extremely negative, we can visualize white light energy coming from our heart centers into theirs. Then see it going up through the top of their heads, up to the sun, and coming back down into the top of our heads, into our hearts and back to them. Circulating this love force is a very powerful tool. It lifts them up. This can be silently done in person or on the phone. It protects our energy from getting drained and uplifts both parties.

Another effective technique is to listen to the person while they are yelling and then, when they're done, ask them, "What's really hurting you?" Let them talk about their pain; this really can help to heal the problem. Many times people just need to express their hurt when they are acting angry on the outside.

I had a profound experience with this technique in the early 1970s. I went to speak at a San Francisco convention celebrating the arrival of the Kohoutek comet. Before I went on, the music was extremely loud and people were dancing up a storm in the main lobby. There were several thousand people attending this event. Someone then made an error of cutting the music off sharply so everyone was rudely interrupted. I sat on a dais with several male spiritual teachers who were dressed as Indian gurus.

There was a man in the audience who began yelling and was extremely rageful at the gurus for presenting themselves as better than everyone else. He was screaming, and before I knew it he was coming up on stage right in front of me. A voice within said, "He's going to kill one of the yogis unless you stop him." I immediately got up and stood face-to-face with him and started pushing out love to this man for all I was worth. No matter what he yelled, I kept saying "I love you. What's the matter? Please let me help you." After two minutes, he stopped, and started crying out that his best friend had just been put in prison that day and he was feeling horrible. I comforted the man, and he calmed down and was led off stage. Projecting the love force is amazingly powerful.

Detachment: How to Stay Centered

After learning to stay centered and calm, we begin to perceive life from a higher spiritual awareness. We become the compassionate observer of all that we do, and understand the lessons of our lives. It's an honest, detached, and non-judgmental place we reside in.

Being detached does not mean we're doormats. It means we'll be honest in our self-expression. If we can't do something for someone, we'll be able to verbalize that. We might say, "You know, that simply does not work for me any more," or "I simply can't do it that way." We set up our new boundaries. If someone wants us to do something that we feel is detrimental or is making us sick, we say, "Absolutely not, I can't do that." But if we don't verbalize our truth, the same problem will keep manifesting in the future, until we get the lesson. We can get really tired of repeating the same lessons.

To be detached also doesn't mean we're acting cold, aloof, or without compassion. Withdrawing or isolating ourselves from others is not part of the centering self-growth process. Detachment is knowing that each of us has his or her unique pathway to growth. Others may take longer or choose not to grow at all. If people don't ask for our help or opinions, it means that they don't want our help or that they're not really ready to grow. It's not our business to decide that it's time for that other person to shape up.

As mystics, when we see someone suffering we feel compassion but we also learn to see people as God-empowered beings who are choosing their lessons. We can share something like, "I wish you'd love yourself more; I think you're wonderful," or "How do you think you set up this situation, what's your positive lesson, and what do you think you can do to change it?" We can ask if they would like a hug or if they would just like to have us listen as they talk about the problem.

If people don't respond to our ideas and suggestions, that's fine, too. We just offer ideas and tools that have helped us, and let them grow where they take root. Sharing our own experiences and solutions we've found useful personally are ways to help a situation. If people choose to seek help, let them know there are also support groups and counselors available to help solve their problems.

Learning to Trust

Spiritual growth is a gradual stepping-beyond process that eliminates our dependence on outside sources for self-esteem and self-value. It's putting total trust in God and ourselves, rather than trying to depend on other people. God is always a receptive, loving powerful force that is consistent in our lives.

Through our past hurts and disappointments, many of us lost our ability to trust others. What we truly mistrust is our own ability to make wise choices. Because of our poor judgments in the past, we assume we are unable to choose wisely now. Realize we can now be more discriminating and can choose people in our lives who deserve our love and trust.

The more we feel connected with the God force, the more we will see our lives as the unfoldment of our greater good. As we see the beauty in this process, we learn to trust it implicitly. We are never alone in this journey, and it is a privilege to learn and grow in this process.

Coping with Endings

At the first signs of difficulty, couples should seek help from professional counselors, or openly discuss and look at their own problems together. All too often, couples wait until the love has died before they seek help. If one of the partners refuses to go for help or to communicate, the other cannot keep the marriage going alone. If both partners know within their hearts that they have tried everything humanly possible to save the marriage and cannot overcome the difficulties, then it's time to end the partnership.

When leaving marriages where there are children involved, we need to be especially supportive in explaining to the children that our decision to be apart has nothing to do with them. Our love for them will always be there. Explain to them that even though adults may love one another, they may not be able to live together in harmony. It's important that we don't ever try to use the children as weapons to get back at our spouses.

If our partners continue to choose to stay depressed, compulsively addicted, or abusive, we may need to separate ourselves from them. We can't stay around to watch them self-destruct if it starts to destroy our well-being. We have to protect our own energy. Explain that we love them but that it hurts us too much to watch them hurt themselves.

If it is time for us to part company from certain people, realize that we are who we are today because of the lessons each of these people came into our lives to teach us. Bless them for what they have taught us about ourselves. Don't see the endings of relationships as failures. They teach us to be more self-loving and responsible in our choices for the future. Also, spend time reviewing what roles or patterns contributed to the tension and problems in the relationship. If we don't get the lesson, then we'll set up someone else to come in and teach it to us.

It's important that we take care of ourselves during these life transitions. Endings can cause up and down energy swings as we are adjusting to the change. We need to get outdoors, get plenty of exercise, fresh air, and good food, and make it a point to be around happy and creative people. We need to put our energy into a new creative project, class, or activity that feeds energy back into us. Think of this particular period as a time of self-evaluation and a splendid opportunity for working through some of the most important lessons of our lives.

Remember that the secret of a happy marriage is communication. This means communicating not only our joys and pleasures, but also our fears and insecurities. Anything not shared can become a block. When we can share our negative programs (as well as our positive ones) in a spirit of trust, looking at them and changing them, we can grow very fast indeed.

The true marriage relationship has seldom been tried. It remains a frontier of love and freedom within our own inner being, and still awaits our exploration.

■ *Qualities of Love* Worksheets

If God seems far away, guess who moved?
                                        —Anonymous

I. Reflect on your daily meditation practice this week. What was your experience of meditation? How did it effect your energy this week?

_____

_____

_____

_____

II. Write down a dream from this week. What did you learn about yourself from this dream?

_____

_____

_____

III. What affirmations and visualizations are you using? How did you do with hearing your negative thoughts, cancelling them, and putting in a positive affirmation instead?

_____

_____

_____

Relationship Affirmation: "Divine Love is present in all my relationships. I give and receive love easily and effortlessly."

IV. Lesson of the Week

Write down at least one positive thing you learned during the past week. Review where you reacted, and look to discover a new way to respond as a self-empowered, loving being:

_____

_____

_____

_____

_____

V. Ten-Step Guide to Improving Relationships

1. Live each day to the fullest. As much as you can, be in the present. At the end of every day forgive yourself and forgive others, and thank Life for another opportunity to learn and love. Avoid living in the past, or basing your happiness upon the achievement of some future goals.

2. Take responsibility for your thoughts and feelings. Speak in "I feel . . ." statements rather than "You are . . ." Pay attention to your feelings—whether positive or negative—because they are telling you valuable information about yourself.

3. Listen to your body. Often we are out of touch with our true feelings or emotions but the body does not lie. Are you stressed, irritated, getting sick? Listen to the body during interactions with others and you will often get a true reading of what is going on with you.

4. To thine own self be true. Be kind and compassionate, yet do not pretend feelings and beliefs that are not there. Honesty is the basis of intimacy—with self and another. Examine the roles you play that are not authentic.

5. Make your own mistakes and give others the same right. Avoid the parent-counselor role of trying to solve another's problems. Be sounding boards for one another, but let the other person solve his or her own problems. That's what you are here for, and it's the only way you will ever grow. You will have all you can do to work on your own stuff.

6. Set up "communication time" and develop some ground rules for discussing problems or difficulties. The things you agree on are easy; it's the things that you disagree on that can drive you up a wall. To effectively problem-solve, each person must learn to adopt an assertive approach, stating what the problem is and what he or she wants, and suggesting a possible fair and workable solution. But most important, each person

needs to practice listening to the other. "You never listen . . . you don't understand me . . ." are all-too-frequent complaints.

7. Loving someone does not mean you will enjoy living with him or her. You may love unconditionally, but you cannot live or work in this world without establishing some ground rules and boundaries. Much needless suffering arises from *assuming* that you both know what the ground rules are. Openly discuss your living, working, or loving agreements.

8. Practice seeing your partner (friend, colleague, employer, etc.) as a fully empowered person, free to make his or her own choices. Yet practice acknowledging that each of us is here because "God isn't finished with us yet." Each person has strengths and weaknesses. Take others off pedestals. Recognize that everyone has many different aspects.

9. Remind yourself that expecting others to constantly meet your emotional, mental, and physical needs will result in continual frustration. Practice creating a sense of fullness and completeness from within. "I have all the love I need within my own heart." Practice meeting others from a feeling of confidence and wholeness, rather than a feeling of need or insecurity.

10. Daily cultivate your own spiritual resources. Develop your intuition, your higher awareness, and keep your energy high. How your world works is up to you.

VI. Through this course you have been able to identify some of the limiting programs in your thinking. How do these programs presently affect your closest relationships?

VII. Being honest with others sends out a message that you can love yourself and deserve to be loved by others. Sometimes we feel resentment towards others because we didn't verbalize our boundaries.

Give an example of a situation this week where you did not verbalize your true feelings. What was the result?

_____

_____

_____

_____

Now give an example where you did verbalize your true feelings. What was the result?

_____

_____

_____

_____

VIII. Compliments and Criticism Time

This is a thirty-minute exercise to be done with a partner, friend, or relative to improve your communication skills. For the first ten minutes, one person shares all his or her thoughts, feelings, and problems concerning the relationship, while the other person just listens. For the second ten minutes, trade roles and the previous listener now gets to share without being interrupted. Then for the last ten minutes, both people share and discuss their thoughts

and feelings together. I recommend this as a weekly exercise for
partners. Try this and write down your experience:

_____

_____

_____

_____

_____

_____

IX. What are five of your greatest strengths and weaknesses that
presently affect your closest relationships?

Strengths   *Weaknesses*

1. _____   1. _____

2. _____   2. _____

3. _____   3. _____

4. _____   4. _____

5. _____   5. _____

X. What qualities are you attracted to in others? Which ones do you
tend to react to?

_____

_____

_____

_____

XI. What qualities do you offer in relationships?

_____

_____

_____

XII. How do you picture yourself in your ideal relationship? What
roles, qualities, and characteristics would you like to see?

_____

_____

_____

_____

XIII. If you are in a heart-to-heart intimate relationship, list two ways you might be holding back from opening to receive more love. If you're not in such a relationship, list two ways you might be blocking yourself from leading in a partner:

_____

_____

_____

_____

XIV. List one person who has provided your most important or challenging relationship in each of the following categories. Next to each name, write down what positive lesson he or she has taught you about your self-love (or lack of it!):

1. Spouse/Partner_____

2. Friend_____

3. Relative_____

4. Boss/Co-worker _____

5. Children _____

XV. Guided Visualization

In this exercise, I want you to think of someone that you're really having problems with, or someone who has hurt you very badly and with whom you have not been able to clear the problem.

Imagine yourself walking through a luscious forest . . . You're coming up on a small hillside, with beautiful trees, and the sun is filtering through . . . It's a beautiful day. All you can hear is the sound of the birds . . . As you're walking along, you come to a wonderful waterfall with a little creek going down it, and a bridge crossing the creek . . . Sit down on a rock and listen to the water. Listen to the sounds. It's so beautiful, and so peaceful . . .

As you're sitting there very relaxed, I want you to imagine, coming up the path on the opposite side of the stream, this person that you've had a great deal of difficulty with . . . See this person as five years old—not as an adult, but as a five-year-old child . . . See him or her sitting down on the other side of the bridge . . . Ask this person, "What was I learning from my experience with you? What is my positive lesson from our relationship?" . . . And imagine the child's soul answering you . . .

Now imagine the child running across the bridge and hugging you, and you both start laughing at what wonderful teachers you were for each other . . . Isn't it wonderful that you love each other enough to come in and teach one another so that you learn to know ourselves and you can work through these hurts?

Now imagine the child giving you a gift . . . Interpret the gift as you would a dream symbol. What is being handed to you? . . .

And now see yourself giving the child a gift . . . What have you given to the child? . . .

You begin to see how important you both were in one another's lives. For everyone that enters your life is playing a role for you, and you need those roles to be who you are today. How wonderful that you both could come together to learn this!

Embrace the child with love, . . . then release the child . . . It runs back across the bridge and down the path . . . You're free now to go on with your life without ever having to feel the pain or the hurt that you felt before you came to this spot . . .

And any time you have a problem, you can come back here and connect with the person or the situation and ask what the lesson is. It is always, always positive . . .

Now imagine yourself going back down the hillside, . . . back through the forest, . . . Now close your hands into a fist, and open your eyes.

Write down any insights your received from the exercise:

_____

_____

_____

_____

_____

_____

_____

XVI. Assignment for Week 7:

- *Do* your daily twenty-minute meditation.

- *Write* down any dreams you have this week.

- *Practice* daily affirmations and visualizations.

- *Read* Week 7 and fill out the "Congratulations Graduate" worksheets.

Week 7

AWAKENING THE SPIRITUAL SELF

The real voyage of discovery consists not in seeking new landscapes, but in having new eyes.

—Marcel Proust

We Can Make a Difference

We are living in a time of great transition that includes planetary changes as well as changes in humankind's consciousness. It's time to stop, to discover and develop our intuitive gifts, and to create a better world. There is tremendous energy and knowledge available for this process, and it's free for the asking. The condition of the Earth is but a reflection of the state of humankind's mind. This is why the cleaning up of our own negative programs is the greatest gift we can offer for changing and improving the planet.

What we are inside truly affects the world's condition. We can run around endlessly trying to fix the results of everyone's negative thinking, or we can change things at their root—by changing our own thoughts, words, and actions to the positive. Our self-growth and love are also the seeds for inspiring others to do this work. The statement, "By their fruits you shall know them," contains profound wisdom. Getting our own lives in order is the best testament to others of the value of the spiritual process.

Each person can and does make a difference. As long as we've tried to improve ourselves and our world, we have fulfilled our life's purpose. Even if the world continues to turn away from becoming consciously aware, we will still rise to higher realms of existence through our efforts to live and practice love.

Life is Perfect

Even with our spiritual teachings, knowledge of reincarnation, and belief that our lives are perfectly designed, we may still wrestle with our practical reality. We may experience doubt about the spiritual process, the timings of events, and the unexpected outcomes of our experiences. Even though we may not understand difficult situations that occur here, we can ask about them when we cross over into the death state. I've had problems this life believing that children's suffering is part of God's divine plan. I understand that we reap what we sow, but it was still hard for me to accept their condition.

I had a dream one night that helped me to understand that our lives set up on the Earth plane are perfect in the eyes of God. It was in the 1970s, and I was living up in the beautiful Lake Tahoe area of California. In horror I had watched the evening news in which I saw mothers shoving their babies onto a plane leaving Vietnam, in the hopes they could be saved. I had lost my own son in the war there in 1971. I began to feel very guilty, thinking, "Here I am sitting up here in my mountain home, safe and comfortable, while others are suffering so miserably. What am I to do?"

That night, I dreamt I was on a steep mountain; it was the Our Father Ski Run at Alpine Meadows, which angles straight down. I was standing there on skis with a wise old teacher who said to me, "Look up there," and I looked up and saw a skier going straight down the mountainside. The teacher said to me, "Whatever you desire in life, you will have to incarnate to actualize." I knew that he was saying that whatever we desire, we must work through on the Earth plane, so we should be careful what we ask for. Anything that we desire will keep pulling us back into incarnation until we actualize it. So, in the next vision I saw, I was hovering way above the Earth and I saw the perfection of life—this is what is called cosmic consciousness.

It was an amazing sight. Everything in the universe was in absolutely perfect order. When I started to come back to my body, I said, "Oh, please let me bring some of this knowledge with me; I don't want to leave it." It was the most peaceful I had felt in my whole life. The closer I got back to my body, the more the stubborn me came through, and I yelled, "But what about the babies in Vietnam?"

Everything stopped, and the wise man said to me, "You cannot go through life without meeting someone with a chip on their shoulder or an ax to grind. Isn't it perfect that God allows 'Vietnams' for people to get their fill of violence in?" And once again I understood what he was trying to communicate. From God's point of view, this life is our school for learning about ourselves, and our opportunity to unwind our karmic lessons. The world is our stage on which we reflect where we are within ourselves. If we are in conflict within, we will manifest the same in our outer reality.

Stress and Tension: Saboteurs of Well-Being

If we deplete our energy through worry, overworking, improper health management, or lack of self-love, we can get caught up in playing the victim role in life. We will experience the positive results of our growth process through making our spirituality a daily practice. We need to stay in tune with our physical, emotional, mental, and spiritual requirements.

It's important to keep our lives simple. If we get too complicated and diverse with our energy flows, we won't be able to hear our inner voices. Be honest and patient with self and others. Removing perfectionist attitudes and releasing self-limiting programs help to clear the way for achieving peace and serenity within.

Understand that a lack of motivation comes from a lack of energy. With high energy, we'll find that inspiration and motivation go hand in hand with new ideas. Experience each day as a wonderful journey into the unknown, knowing that God is with us every step of the way. The love and support are always there.

The following is a message from my Guidance on *Man as an Energy Being*. Its message continues to inspire me:

As we begin to tune in to the God force of our own beings, we begin to understand the magnificence of this energy. It is only by going within that we can begin to really get answers to our many questions.

Before doing this, if you ask questions and receive answers, regardless of the descriptions we use, you do not have the eyes to see and the ears to hear. Many of your questions cannot be answered in words and understood on the Earth plane level. But as you go within, you intuitively know the answers.

The knowledge comes to you as a state of mind. It is a state beyond language, beyond the intellect. It is only through tuning in to this state of awareness that you will know, not through our lengthy explanations.

It is difficult to teach the power of the God force to the masses, because people think of themselves as separate from one another and from God. As long as you are seeing things as separate instead of as one unit, one power, you cannot possibly understand the meaning of this force, the love of God within you. You are not separate from one another, nor are you separate from the things on the Earth plane which you see.

As you learn to see yourself not as a drop separate from the ocean, but as part of that ocean, you can truly express the totality of your being. You will know how unlimited you are. How can a drop tell you about the power and force of the ocean unless it has united with the ocean and become one with that power?

Your power lies in realizing this Oneness. The force behind the unity is love.

It is very important for individuals to learn to redirect their awareness, to take responsibility for this energy. As people begin to experiment with tuning in to this power and get brief glimpses of it, many become frightened of it. Many pull away for fear of misuse, responsibility, or self-discipline. Few are willing to openly explore and experience this energy, because they are unwilling to discipline themselves enough to do it. But there is nothing to fear, for this power is that of a loving God, a gift that can awaken you to new dimensions of happiness and aliveness.

To accept this gift requires that you have a purpose, a direction for your life, and that you assume the responsibility for your own growth. Yet, for the most part, you continue the merry-go-round of life, reincarnation after reincarnation, never tapping into that which is freely given within the self.

If you understood this power, this energy, you would never have to struggle for peace and harmony, but only attune to that which is within.

Protecting Your Mystical Abilities

It is our responsibility to maintain the care and up-keep of our energy, health, and well-being. There will always be too much to do and people and situations that need help. In our reaching out to help others, we must always balance our own needs with those of others. Maintaining daily meditation, with the closing down at the end, is a must, especially if we are going to work in this high-speed world and in the healing or teaching professions. We have to recharge our energy or we can "burn out" and experience health disorders. It's important to always do an energy check on oneself before taking on extra projects or helping others.

My Guidance has said that people doing intuitive counseling should work two days, then take one day off for rest and play. Also, channeling to get insight from one's teachers should be done only on a weekly basis for a maximum of one hour. Otherwise, the energy use can drain us. If we need more ongoing help from our teachers, we can program for a dream or do a guided visualization exercise.

If we work in the healing arts professions, we need to be sure the energy is being fed back to us to maintain our stability. Begin each session by visually circulating the energy. Imagine it flowing from us to the patient, up to the sun, and then back into us (as described in Week 4 on healing). We each need to be recharged. We can help to heal others, but if they don't take responsibility for the life programs that are setting up the disease, the problem will re-surface until the inner healing work is done.

We need to protect our energy as we tap into higher spiritual energies. As we become more intuitive, psychic, and sensitive, we need to monitor our alcohol intake. Most sensitive people cannot handle alcohol or drugs, as they cause us to leave the body. Then, our eyes can glaze over and a discarnate entity can inhabit our bodies during this time. The reason people can't remember their actions when they "black out" is that they are out of the body.

Drugs can also have a very negative effect on our energy fields. We can lose our grounding and this throws our entire system off balance. Keep an eye on the dosages and effects of prescription drugs as well. We may find that we are much more susceptible to their influence than we suspect, and need to monitor our responses to them and communicate with our doctors about the results.

Maintaining a healthy and balanced program of exercise and diet, and creating time for play and rest, are essential ingredients for our mystical development. It's also useful to increase our meditation time by five to ten minutes when we need extra energy.

Spreading the Light

This is a pivotal time to be alive on Earth. It's time for all of us to let our light shine out to all the people who are led to us. The Earth needs all beings drawn to the light to share their divine inner wisdom and knowledge with the masses.

As we take self-responsibility for our own lives and stop blaming others, the transformation process can occur. This is true on an individual level as well as on a world scale. When cities and countries, as well as powerful leaders, can look within and clean up their own problems, then the world can shift into a new functional order. Racism, sexism, wars, poverty, drugs, and homelessness are all the results of broken lives in a system that has lost its spiritual heritage. At present, humankind seeks to control the world through fear. But fear is the ultimate lack of spiritual awareness. Love is the greatest healing force of all.

People will be led to us when it is time for us to teach. We are each like Johnny Appleseed, spreading out the ideas and tools for the spiritual process. Cast the seeds on fertile soil. This may be through our families, friendships, businesses, or artistic endeavors. Or we may work as healers or spiritual teachers. Each of our pathways will be unique and appropriate for our life's work.

It is a privilege to be a torchbearer of this inner light. In presenting positive divine energy, we can transform the negative vibrations that abound. Love is the strongest force in the universe. The higher our energy, the more people will be drawn to us and the easier our lives will become.

We are not alone in facing the challenges of our earthly lives. We are all teachers and students throughout this journey. We can further nurture ourselves by joining with other like-minded beings in meditations and group activities that support this positive spiritual perspective. Remember, too, that God and our Guidance are always present, ready to assist this process in us.

Graduating from Earth

Many people will not be ready this lifetime to face themselves. God has given each of us free will to do whatever we want in our lifetimes. We can share our experiences with others and be tolerant if they are not ready to listen or change. It's a waste of time to try to help people who aren't interested in their growth.

By the same token, we can take what feels right and discard what doesn't from anyone else as well. On the spiritual path, it's useful to remain an open-minded skeptic. We each know what feels right to us. Release and forgive others who have taught us along the way, and be open to exploring and experiencing new ways of being.

The spiritual growth path is a journey that never ends. When we complete the lessons we set out to finish in this lifetime, we are allowed to ascend to higher levels of existence. We earn the right to study and learn with the spiritual Masters on the other side. The rewards are phenomenal. We can go to great universities and classes, travel to other worlds, and develop creative gifts we may not have had time to develop while on Earth. We can remain as teachers from the other side, or choose to reincarnate again to help serve others. We are given great freedom to explore and experience the divine pleasures of being a true force of light and love. Myself, I want to be on a dream team and develop great dream ideas for people to help them with their growth, and watch them from the other side.

I really believe that this is the most exciting time for humankind. I see that through the experiences, changes, and lessons before us, we will begin to take more self-responsibility and make this world a better place in which to live. This is why it's so important for each us to shine our light and contribute whatever talents, gifts, and abilities we possess. It doesn't matter how big or small the contribution, it only matters that we each try to contribute. As we learn to love and accept ourselves unconditionally, we can learn to love our fellow beings in the same way. Rejoice at the great opportunity for this new transformation!

■ *Congratulations Graduate* Worksheets

The best way to know God is to love many things.
—Vincent Van Gogh

I. Reflect on your daily meditation practice during this course. What results and differences have you seen in your life from doing this practice?

II. Look over your dream journal for the last six weeks. What did you learn about yourself from your dreams?

_____

_____

_____

_____

_____

III. What affirmations and visualizations will you continue to use in your life?

_____

_____

_____

_____

IV. **Lesson of the Week**

Write down at least one positive thing you learned during the past week. Review where you reacted, and look to discover a new way to respond as a self-empowered, loving being.

_____

_____

_____

_____

V. What areas in your life still need improvement?

_____

_____

_____

_____

_____

VI. What tools or techniques will you use to help transform these areas?

_____

_____

_____

_____

_____

VII. Take some time to review your answers from Weeks 2 and 3. Where have you made progress in these areas?

_____

_____

_____

_____

VIII. How has your energy level changed since working on this workbook?

_____

_____

_____

_____

_____

IX. How can you encourage greater creativity, joy, and play in your life in the weeks to come?

_____

_____

_____

_____

X. In what ways will you continue to strengthen your spiritual growth and awareness in the weeks and months to come?

_____

_____

_____

_____

XI. How has your trust in your inner guidance increased during the last six weeks?

_____

_____

_____

_____

XII. In what ways have you found it easiest to receive insight (dreams, guided visualizations, hearing the inner voice, people's ideas, etc.)?

_____

_____

_____

_____

XIII. Which week's topics did you find the easiest to write about? Which was the toughest? Why?

_____

_____

_____

_____

_____

XIV. If you were your Master teacher, what advice would you give yourself on how to love yourself more?

_____

_____

_____

_____

XV. Guided Visualization

You've gone through the day-to-day steps of really starting to look at your true purpose and the meaning of life, and you're seeing them differently than you ever saw them before. You have learned many important lessons and insights about yourself in the past six weeks. In learning to perceive the beauty and the good within yourself, you are now able to see the good within all people. This offers you great freedom and joy to experience life.

Now here's a visualization to celebrate your wonderful self-growth work and graduation:

Close your eyes and imagine yourself sitting in a beautiful golden temple . . . The lights are on, and there are angelic voices ringing out in song . . . This is your graduation . . . Imagine yourself walking down the aisle while everyone is singing, walking up to the front of the church, where you see Jesus standing . . . Buddha is also standing there . . . Mohammed is there, and all the great Master teachers are standing on the stage, facing you . . . They're cheering you on . . . You have begun your path . . . It is an important path, and you are very loved for having started this search . . .

And as you walk up, you will stand in front of a teacher . . . You may choose any one you want . . . And imagine the teacher putting over your head a beautiful golden necklace . . . And on that is a gold key . . . This key is there for you to use any time, any place, for the rest of your life . . . Any time you have a problem, imagine the key hanging on your necklace and picture yourself sitting on a throne of gold in this temple. Then sit there and await your teachers' presence . . . They will always come . . . The answers will be given.

Even if you cannot hear the answer, you will feel their love, strength, and support . . . All you ever have to do is ask to receive; it will always be given to you. Sometimes you may be are too tired or weary to hear. That's when you receive the support, the love, the wisdom, the knowledge . . . But it's in the asking that the key opens the door to giving you the truth and the answers . . .

Now imagine yourself embracing the teacher with whom you feel most comfortable. And as you embrace him or her, feel the tremendous surge of energy as your body lights up . . .

Never limit yourself to this one teacher, for many will come as you raise your energy, but know this one as a door-keeper for you. Your teachers will be there throughout your lifetime as friends, as supports, and as beings who will help you through the stages of your development . . .

Feel their presence, and now see them . . . You are all one in the beautiful divine energy of love . . . Now return to the room, close your hands into a fist, and open your eyes.

Write down any insights you received from the exercise:

When you're tuning in and you want answers, go to the highest source. You can always ask for help in these exercises. When asking important questions, you can always go to God Himself. You have access to tap in to Jesus, Buddha, or anyone you choose. All you have to do is ask. This being can be a friendly teacher, a friendly guide along the road of life. And as your gifts develop and you go forward, you will be as a teacher for others who are drawn into your light. And this is as it should be.

In helping others, in helping yourself, you are actually helping the masses. And this spreads like a fire throughout the land, consuming all hatred, judgment, and fear, and leaves only love in its place, and fresh new growth.

Be proud of yourself, for the effort that you've put into this course. Understand that each time you meditate, you're increasing the light, love, and level of spiritual energy for yourself and the planet. Your growth process may seem challenging at times, but it gets easier the more you practice, practice, practice. Your dreams, insights, and self-awareness will come more easily as you continue the process. You will not be disappointed. The rewards are extraordinary.

Congratulations on Your Self-Growth Process and Completing the Workbook—Keep up the Good Work!

Epilogue

KNOWING AND LOVING YOURSELF

A Message from Betty Bethards' Guidance

The purpose of the earthly incarnation is solely to know yourself. To know yourself means to love all parts of yourself—the weaknesses as well as the strengths. It means looking at the self-imposed limitations and the limitations you let others put on you.

God does not ask that you be perfect—no person need be perfect, on our side, as well as on yours. We ask only that you learn to be honest with yourself by evaluating the lessons that you're going through. Then your life and your presence have a more positive and unique effect on the Earth plane.

If you could love yourself completely and see the beauty that is within you, you would begin to see the beauty in others, and the world would transform around you. You must work to know yourself, to see your own unlimited beauty, power, and abilities. Then you will find beauty in everyone else.

Just as there are no two people with the same thumb-print, there are no two people whose gifts are alike. Each of you has something special to offer the world. It's in sharing that you begin to see the joy and the beauty of loving yourselves and loving all others without judging them. Since you have not walked in another's shoes, you do not know what their lessons may be. Concentrate on your own lessons and let no one weaken you by making your decisions and doing your work for you.

As long as you are meditating and as long as you are working with your dreams, you have your direct line to your own Guidance, and to God. Each and every day, you are awakened to new insights, new perspectives, new ways of dealing with problems. You become more creative in solving your problems. Worry over unresolved problems always drains your energy.

From the moment you step into your Earth suit until the time you leave at death, there is something to be learned and experienced. Your teachers are always loving and supportive of your journey. You are never alone. Excitement and joy come from creatively resolving each problem, gaining the insight, and moving ahead in self-understanding. Remember that every so-called problem is really bringing a gift of insight to you.

How simple it is to take the time to know yourself. Meditation is the gift of love that nourishes you and allows the God energy to flood into your being. By meditating daily, you'll be moving toward having all wisdom, knowledge, and truth. If you will, imagine a huge mountain with everyone walking all around, no two people taking the same path. Yet all are engulfed in a beautiful golden light as they go toward the summit of the mountain.

By meditating, you begin to see yourself as one among many fellow travelers, all taking different roads, all going to the same mountaintop. We're all learning in our own way and in our own time. How wonderful it is that there is not just one path to the mountaintop! The beauty in coming together and sharing our experience with others is that we can all grow and learn from one another.

As you wander up the mountain of life, you may have to retrace your steps many times. Know that you are on the journey, and you can make it faster and more enjoyable by not retracing too many steps. Knowing yourself means that you're lightening your load, and the going gets easier and easier the further you go. You cannot pull anyone else with you, for each person must walk his own path on his own two feet. Enjoy the comfort and the society of those who are sharing paths that are the same as or similar to yours, and lovingly release those who are not.

See your own inner beauty and keep walking forward. As you begin to gain a broader perspective and glimpse the humor that we see as we look at your struggles, your mountains will begin to seem more like molehills. As you climb the mountain of enlightenment, the journey will get steeper if you make it difficult for yourself. Yet you can fly on the wings of love and ascend to the top without your feet ever touching the ground, if you fly with your teachers and let them help you on your journey. It can be an adventure of great joy and pleasure.

Stop to look at the things around you. Enjoy the sunsets, enjoy the oceans and all of nature's majesty. There is amazing beauty and energy that is free to all for the taking. You can look at the same beauty in one another. As you look for that beauty, you're seeing through the eyes of love.

Seeing through the eyes of love means seeing as God sees you. You're seeing as your Guidance and your soul see you. The soul is gently patient and understands the lessons you chose to learn. Open your eyes and see! Open your hearts and love! Feel and know as God knows! Learn to listen and go within to hear the insight that is given to you. Great truths are also given to you in the dream state. The answers and messages are always there.

Life is eternal. These are eternal lessons. The excitement comes each day. Live one day at a time. See what gifts are presented to you through observing your reactions to things and situations and dealing with those reactions. This will keep you busy for your whole life.

Love yourselves, bless yourselves, and pray for yourselves. Send out love and light, and live what you believe. God bless you!

Additional Reading

The following is a list of other useful books by Betty Bethards for helping you to develop your spiritual and intuitive abilities. As you explore the many books and teachings in the self-growth field, the authors recommend you look for those works which are simple, positive, self-empowering, and speak the truth to your soul.

From Element Books

- *The Dream Book: Symbols for Self-Understanding*

From The Inner Light Foundation

- *Be Your Own Guru*
- *Relationships in the New Age of AIDS*
- *Sex and Psychic Energy*
- *Techniques for Health and Wholeness*
- *There is No Death*
- *Way to Awareness*

- 30 Cassette Tapes

For more information on Betty's lectures, seminars, books, and tapes, please send a self-addressed stamped envelope to:

Inner Light Foundation
P.O. Box 750265
Petaluma, CA 94975
Phone: (707) 765-2200